Six
Action
Shoes

Six
Action
Shoes

Edward de Bono

HarperBusiness
A Division of HarperCollins*Publishers*

Library of Congress Cataloging-in-Publication Data

de Bono, Edward, 1933–
    Six action shoes / Edward de Bono.
        p.   cm.
    ISBN 0–88730–513–X
    1. Management.   I. Title.
    HD31.D4213   1991
    658—dc20
                                                    91–15813
                                                        CIP
Printed in the United States of America
91 92 93 94 JL/RRD 9 8 7 6 5 4 3 2 1

Contents

Author's Note
Thinking and Action

Very few people just sit and think. Most of us eventually take action. You might think of something to buy at the supermarket, but then you buy it. You might plan a new strategy for an electronics company, but then you implement the strategy. Often we assume that action is easy and obvious—that thinking lays out the roads and decides which road is to be taken and that action is as simple as walking along the correct road. It's not that easy. Some people do seem to have a natural flair for action, just as some people have a flair for thinking and for creativity. Such people benefit greatly from some additional training. For those without a flair training is essential.

I spend a great deal of time in the education world and am involved with the largest program in the world for the direct teaching of thinking in schools (the CoRT Thinking Programme*). Too often education is about description and analysis. That is the academic tradition, and they are easier to teach than teaching how to act. But the real world involves *action* as well as knowledge. That is why I invented the word *operacy*, which is the skill of action. The word *operacy* has the same base as the word *operations*. Operacy is just as important as literacy and numeracy.

---

*The CoRT Thinking Programme is published by S.R.A., Chicago, educational publishers.

This book has very much to do with operacy. The framework of the six action shoes is a help both in the training of action skills and also in the use of those skills at the moment of action.

"Be perfect," "Do the right thing," are instructions that are easy to give—but such instructions have little practical value. By breaking down action into six distinct modes, the six action shoe framework gives specific guidance about the action that needs to be taken. When you cook, you choose your ingredients. In action you can choose your action style to fit the needs of the occasion.

This book was written on a flight from London, England, to Auckland, New Zealand. It was written on a Psion MC400 mobile computer. I have included in the text my notes regarding the position of the plane, etc., during the writing. There is no special value to these notes, but they give a sense of immediacy to the book. Needless to say, the material in this book had been thought about for a long time. 👣

Introduction

THE PLACE IS A SMALL MEETING ROOM IN A hotel in Tokyo. The time is eight o'clock in the morning on 6 December 1986. I am giving a short talk on the Japanese translation of my book *Six Thinking Hats*, and the audience is made up of senior Japanese business executives. Among them is Hisashi Shinto, later chosen as Japanese businessperson of the year, and chief executive of Nippon Telephone and Telegraph (NTT), which at that time had 350,000 employees. In stock market valuation, NTT is by far the most highly valued corporation in the world. At that time the total value of the top five U.S. corporations was less than that of NTT. Mr. Shinto liked the idea of the *six thinking hats* and ordered several thousand copies of the book for his executives to read. Some months later I again met Mr. Shinto, who told me that the book had had a powerful effect on his executives. He invited me to talk to the board of management of NTT and also to its top 140 managers.

The framework of the *six thinking hats* has been adopted by many major corporations around the world. The method forms part of the training offered by IBM to its 40,000 managers worldwide in 1990 and is widely used by Prudential Insurance of Canada and the United States. Du Pont, the leading chemical company in the world, uses the method widely, and so does American Standard. Many other corporations (such as Chevron Oil) find this framework useful. Nor is the use of the six hat framework restricted to business. The method is increasingly used in education.* The nine-year-old students at Norfolk Academy made a short video showing the use of the six hats; the video was so good that it later was used in training naval personnel.

The six hat method has been widely accepted because it is simple, it is practical, and it works. It actually changes how thinking takes place in meetings and elsewhere: instead of the usual to and fro arguments it makes it possible for people to have constructive discussions.

The method is simple. There are six imaginary hats, each of a different color. At any moment a thinker may choose to put on one of the hats or may be asked to put on or take off a hat. All people at a meeting can use a hat of a particular color for a few moments at a time. The hats involve participants in a type of mental role playing.

White hat: An objective look at data and information

Red hat: Legitimizes feelings, hunches, and intuition

Black hat: Logical negative, judgment, and caution

Yellow hat: Logical positive, feasibility, and benefits

Green hat: New ideas and creative thinking

Blue hat: Control of the thinking process

---

*Education version published by Perfection Learning, Des Moines, Iowa.

The method may seem extremely simple and even childish—but it does work. It works because it sets the rules of the game, and people then can be asked to play the game. People feel foolish if they don't seem to be able to follow the rules. Here are some of the benefits of the method:

- Is simple to learn and use and has an immediate appeal. The visualization of the hats and the colors helps.

- Makes time available for deliberate creative effort. You can ask for "three minutes of green hat thinking."

- Allows the legitimate expression of feelings and intuition in a meeting—without apology or justification: "This is my feeling."

- Allows an "unbinding" of thinking so that each mode gets full attention. It avoids the confusion of trying to do everything at once.

- Provides a simple and direct way of switching thinking without causing offense: "What about some yellow hat thinking here?"

- Requires all thinkers to be able to use each of the hats instead of sticking to only one type of thinking.

- Separates ego from performance in thinking. Frees able minds to examine a subject more fully.

- Provides a practical method for using the different aspects of thinking in the best possible sequence.

- Gets away from to and fro arguments and allows parties to collaborate on constructive exploration.

- Makes for much more productive meetings.

In the traditional argument ("I am right and you are wrong") we seek to explore a subject by presenting and challenging different points of view. The purpose is to challenge everything that is said to arrive at the truth. Those taking part in the discussion become more interested in point scoring, defending their own point of view, and demolishing an opposing point of view than in exploring the subject. Thinking becomes destructive rather than constructive.

By contrast, in the six hat method there is collaborative exploration. Thinking is done in parallel. If the yellow hat is being used, then everyone at the meeting makes an effort to find points of value and benefit in the suggestion. Even those who are against the idea are required to make this effort. It is fascinating to see how much constructive thinking gets done in this way.

Everyone at the meeting may be asked to put on a particular hat: "Let's have some green hat thinking on this."

An individual may be asked to put on a hat: "I want your black hat thinking on this proposal."

People may be asked to take off a hat: "What I have heard so far is red hat thinking. I suggest we take off our red hats."

A person may signal that he or she is putting on a specific hat: "Putting on my green hat I want to put forward a provocation"; "Putting on my red hat this is what I feel"; "Putting on my black hat these are the dangers."

The hats are most effective in occasional use—using one hat at a time in order to obtain a certain type of thinking. When there is a need to explore a subject fully and effectively, a sequence of hats may be put together and then each hat used in turn: "I suggest we start with the white hat and then move on to the green hat. . . ." The blue hat is used to lay out such sequences, to comment on the thinking that is taking place, to summarize what has been thought, and to reach conclusions.

The advantage of the six hat method* is that it is simple and easy to learn and it does work.

The subject of this book—the six pairs of action shoes—follows directly from the six hat framework. 👣

---

*Published as a book by Penguin Books (United Kingdom, Canada, Australia, etc.) and by Little, Brown and Company (United States) and as a book and audio program by ICCT, New York.

PART I
Six Pairs of Action Shoes

Hats suggest thinking. Our many sayings like "Put on your thinking cap (or hat)" were the inspiration for my choice of the hat metaphor for thinking modes. Another reason I chose that metaphor is that a hat is simple to put on and take off. I wanted to emphasize that everyone should be able to put on or take off any one of the hats at a moment's notice. The six modes were *not* six different categories or types of people. Indeed, the purpose of the six hat method is to get away from having people say, "I am the black hat thinker around here" or "Let's have a green thinker in the team." Everyone must be able to use each hat and must make an effort to do so when asked.

But thinking is only one side of things. The other side is action.

Occasionally, thinking is an end in itself, but usually the purpose of thinking is to choose or design a course of action. Sometimes there is a distinct thinking phase and then an action phase. At other times thinking and action are intertwined so that thinking takes place in the course of the action.

Shoes imply action. If you're not walking anywhere, then you don't need shoes. Shoes, like action, are for reaching a destination. Shoes are to action what hats are to thinking. The great success of the six hat thinking framework suggested to me that there is an equal need for a framework for action. Situations require different styles of action. The delicate action needed to paint an eggshell is different from the action needed in a boxing match.

CHAPTER 1

Six Pairs of Action Shoes

The Perfect Person

I had lunch with two senior police officers who were talking about the increasing pressures being felt by the police force. On one side there was increasing crime, violence, drug-related offenses, and criminals who were more and more sophisticated. On the other side the public was putting more and more pressure on the police to behave compassionately. Not only was emergency action required from the police responding to earthquakes, fires, etc., but the police were being asked to perform the roles formerly played by doctors and priests in communities that were small and stable.

All those involved in training police officers were aware that the end product of the training was to be a perfect person who knew how to act appropriately in any type of situation. But how do you get a perfect person? How do you train perfection? That was the problem. Of course, people occasionally approach this ideal. But how can more people attain that state of perfection?

There seem to be two traditional approaches to this problem:

Method 1: Establish rigid codes of behavior and expect people to learn these codes and follow them without deviation. This method avoids the need to think out a response to individual situations. To some extent this used to be the military approach. But how do you establish routines that cover all possible situations? How do people choose between a multitude of routines or act when there is no relevant routine to apply? The effect can be disastrous if the wrong routine is selected. The method works only within a limited range of situations under close supervision.

Method 2: Establish general guiding principles, and then allow people to design their own actions around these principles. This method allows the action to fit the occasion. The guiding principles are designed chiefly to avoid mistakes, and training consists of showing how people follow or fail to follow these guiding principles. There is merit in this approach, but if the principles are very detailed, it is impossible to remember them all, and if the principles are very broad, then they don't give much guidance.

Exhorting someone to behave in a perfect manner is not very useful. We may fool ourselves into believing that we are achieving our objective, but at most we are making only slight improvements. IBM has a slogan that says ''Think.'' This may get people to stop, pause, think, reflect, and appreciate the value of thinking, but its value is limited because the basic instruction—to think—does not in any way explain how this is to be done. The six hat method, simple as it is, does provide a framework for thinking. The six action shoe method does the same for action.

In the course of this discussion on training the perfect person it occurred to me that instead of training one perfect person we should train *six people*, each of whom would be perfect for just one type of situation.

This seemed far more practical and easier to do. Of course, these six people would all live under one skin. That was the origin of the six pairs of action shoes.

The success of the six hat thinking framework suggested that something similar could be done for action. The *need* for perfectly appropriate action suggested a need for breaking down action into six different styles, each of which could be developed. ▮▮

6:26 P.M. U.K. TIME: FLYING OVER SCOTLAND AT 33,000 FEET AND 860 KILOMETERS PER HOUR. SUNSHINE ABOVE SCATTERED CLOUDS. PAUSE FOR DINNER.

PART II
Six Styles of
Action

No ONE IS TAUGHT TO BE A PERFECT COOK instantly. The trainee cook is taught how to deal with soups, then sauces, then meats, and then pastries. Each of these foods has a different action need and requires a different style of cooking. Some cooks always remain better at one type of cooking than at another: there is no reason to suppose that the pastry cook is going to excel at preparing fish. A talented musician may be able to switch from classical music to jazz, from folk music to rock; the trick is to learn the idiom and style of each type of music.

The same holds true for the six pairs of action shoes. Each pair of action shoes is assigned a different color and covers one particular style or idiom of action. Because the style is separated out from general action by the shoe color, it is now possible to learn that style as such. It is possible to get a feel for that style of action. It is possible to become comfortable in a style just as a musician may be comfortable playing jazz.

People don't learn foreign languages in a general sense: they learn Spanish, French, Japanese, or German separately. Once a second or third language is learned, the speaker can switch into that language as the need arises.

So, too, can action styles be focused on separately. A person can become familiar with each of the six different action styles. Action now becomes a two-step process:

Step 1: Ask, ''What type of action is required here?''

Step 2: Put on the appropriate action shoes, and behave in that style.

CHAPTER 2

Six Styles of Action
The Feel of a Situation

The *feel* of a situation is all important. This feel is based
on experience and also on perception. You can predict
how a friend will behave because you know your
friend. When you are with your friend, you slip into
the appropriate behavior. The six action shoes provide
a framework through which a person can become
familiar with different types of situations and then use
this familiarity to react suitably in similar situations.

The mind sees what it is prepared to see and
notices what it is ready to notice. The brain works as a
self-organizing system in which information arranges
itself into patterns—not unlike rain on a landscape
organizing itself into streams and rivers. Experience
follows these patterns just as rain follows the streams
created by previous rainfalls. Once the patterns are
there then we see the world through these patterns.
The six shoe framework provides a set of patterns
through which we can see the world, making it easier
for us to recognize situations and to act effectively.

Many police forces have a code for situations so
that communication can be simplified ("We have a
forty-five here"). This useful shorthand sets up both
expectations and action patterns. The codings describe
the nature of the situation but not the action required.
The six shoe framework indicates the type of behavior
that may be needed in a situation.

CHAPTER 3

Six Styles of Action

Two Shoes in a Pair

We wear only one hat at a time, but there are two shoes in a pair. This turns out to be an advantage. With the six thinking hats we want to do only one thing at a time—like carrying a torch and directing the torch beam in one direction at a time. With action, however, we have to respond to a particular situation without pretending that it is something that we would like it to be.

Situations are rarely pure. They often require a combination of two types of action shoe. So we specify one shoe of each type:

"We have a mixture of orange (emergency) and pink (compassion) here."

"Let's have some grey sneaker action with a touch of brown brogue."

"This is mainly navy shoe routine, but there is some purple stuff too."

Having two shoes in a pair provides flexibility: six shoes have fifteen possible combinations. It isn't necessary to learn the fifteen combinations—only to learn the six types of action and then combine them as required, the way a painter combines basic colors to produce other colors.

CHAPTER 4

Six Styles of Action

Colors for the Shoes

The colors for the shoes must differ from those chosen
for the six thinking hats so that an organization can
use both aspects of the system without confusion. The
colors also have to be normal, everyday colors, which
everyone recognizes. Finally, the color chosen for each
action must suggest the nature of that mode, as was
the case with the six thinking hats:

White hat (information): White as in paper, computer printout. Paper is neutral and carries information.

Red hat (feelings): Red as in fire. Red for warm. The
red hat covers feelings, emotions, and intuition:
"the fires within."

Black hat (logical negative): Black robes worn by a
judge. The judge assesses matters with stern
caution and no nonsense.

Yellow hat (logical positive): Sunshine and optimism.
You feel positive in the sunshine.

Green hat (creative thinking): Green for nature and
for vegetation. Green for growth, shoots, energy.
New ideas spring up.

Blue hat (control of thinking): Blue for sky and
overview. Looking down on the thinking. Blue is
cool and detached.

The choice of colors for the six pairs of action shoes also reflects the nature of each type of shoe, as I show in the next section.

CHAPTER 5

Six Styles of Action

Physical Nature of the Shoes

The shape of the six thinking hats doesn't matter. I use the symbolic top hat, even though top hats are rarely worn today. All hats are the same shape, in fact, because the color makes the difference. Like color, the physical nature indicates the nature of the shoe. Hats are a type of fantasy, but action is more practical. So the physical nature and shape of the shoe are important for visualization and learning purposes but don't need to be mentioned once the framework has been learned.

Visualizing the action shoes, in color and shape, is an important part of the learning process.

Six Styles of Action

The Shoes

The following overview outlines the different colors and shapes of the six action shoes.

Navy formal shoes: Dark blue or navy blue is the color of many uniforms. Navy blue suggests the navy itself, with its drills and routines and formality. In the days of sailing lives depended on correct drills and routines. So the navy shoe action mode covers routines and formal procedures.

Grey sneakers: Grey suggests grey cells and grey matter in the brain. Grey also suggests fog and mist and the difficulty of seeing clearly. The grey sneaker action mode is concerned with exploration, investigation, and collection of evidence. The purpose of the action is to get information.

Brown brogues: Brown is a practical color. Brown suggests earth and basics and feet solidly standing on the earth. Brown also suggests mud and messy situations that are not clearly defined. Brogues are practical hard-wearing shoes that can be used for tough work. So the brown brogue action mode involves practicality and pragmatism. Do what is sensible and what is practical. Figure it out as you go using initiative, practical behavior, and flexibility. In this sense the brown brogue action mode is almost the opposite of the formality of the navy shoes.

Orange gumboots: Orange suggests danger, explosions, attention, warning. The gumboots suggest fire fighters and rescue workers, and the orange gumboot action mode suggests danger and emergency. Emergency action is required. Safety is a prime concern.

Pink slippers: Pink suggests warmth and tenderness. Pink is a conventionally feminine color suggesting home, domesticity, and comfort. Pink is a gentle color. So the pink slipper action mode suggests care, compassion, and attention to human feelings and sensitivities.

Purple riding boots: Purple was the color of imperial Rome. Purple suggests authority. The riding boots also suggest someone riding a horse or at least a motorcycle. The suggestion is of authority. The purple riding boot action mode means playing out the role given by virtue of a position or authority. There is an element of leadership and command. The person is not acting in his or her own capacity but in an official role.

The shoe colors differ from the hat colors. They are everyday colors that suggest the nature of the action mode that they indicate. The physical nature of the shoes also suggests the nature of the action mode.

As I have already indicated, once the framework has been learned and visualized, then there is no need to repeat the whole description of the action mode each time:

''Go in there with a bit of purple.''

"You never were much good at the pink action mode. But it is important. You've got to realize that."

"This is definitely brown mode. We'll figure out as we go along. Be practical and sensible."

"Remember, it's orange."

PART III
Navy Formal Shoes

"Listen, there is a routine. Don't try to figure it out each time. You will surely make mistakes. Stick to the routine. It's navy shoe action mode."

"We are pretty sure he is guilty, but he got off on a technicality. That is what routines are for. Go through the routine automatically. Navy action mode—that's what it's for."

"He charmed you. You forgot to check him out. We have a routine to prevent that. When routines are needed, use them. Navy shoe action mode. Do you understand?"

In the old days life at sea was complicated. Furling sails during a storm was a dangerous procedure that required the coordination of all sailors. Without coordination a sail could break loose and hurl men to their deaths in the sea. The firing of navy guns required formal procedures to avoid guns that exploded or fired too soon. New recruits had to be brought up to speed quickly. The need for discipline led to the establishment of routines.

Many people are irritated by routine because routines tend to stifle initiative and creativity and make for inflexibility. But sometimes routines help us to avoid making dangerous mistakes. It is easier to use a routine checklist than to figure everything out each time.

A person looking out of the control tower at London Airport through a pair of binoculars once noticed that a jumbo jet was attempting to land with its wheels still retracted. The crew allegedly forgot to lower the wheels. The pilot was immediately alerted by radio, and a potential disaster avoided. Routines help us avoid this type of problem. Airlines develop comprehensive checklist routines covering departures and landings. These checklists are improved through experience.

Doctors go through diagnostic routines with their patients to be sure that they have covered all disease possibilities.

I check in and out of nearly a hundred hotels every year, and one of my concerns is that I might leave behind something that I will need later. Insurance can cover the cost of replacing a lost item, but it doesn't take away the inconvenience of not having something (maybe a vital document) when I need it. I've developed a routine of looking in every drawer before I check out of a room. Each time I go through this routine I feel that it is unnecessary because I *know* that I did not use all the drawers. But again and again I have found something vital in a drawer that I knew I had never opened. Now I have set up a further routine. When I check into a hotel, I never use more than the top two dresser drawers so that I know where I have placed things. But I still use the old routine of checking every drawer, as well—just in case the housekeeper stores something in another drawer.

Many a criminal has gone free because an error occurred during the arrest—perhaps the criminal was not read his or her rights. On the one hand, this routine protects those arrested who may not know their rights; on the other hand, failure to go through this routine defeats the purpose of justice.

Society, and most organizations, need rules, laws, procedures, and routines and would find themselves in confusion and chaos without them. Automobile drivers can't choose on which side of the road to drive and what to do at crossroads. Standard forms and routines simplify life and cope with complexity.

At the same time a stifling bureaucracy sometimes seems to exist solely to keep itself in existence. When everything has to be done strictly according to procedures, flexibility and pragmatism are sacrificed. Without set routines the gifted and most capable would certainly do better, but everyone else probably would do worse. The least able would be completely lost. On any occasion a client would have to rely on the personal judgment of a bureaucrat. Corruption would be rampant.

Computers use routines in order to communicate with each other and so do people in an organization.

Routines play a large part in religions because they provide frameworks for worship even when faith is low. Such routines provide continuity. It may be no accident that heavily ritualized religions tend to succeed (Catholicism, Judaism, Islam, Hinduism).

Food is good and essential, but some people overeat and threaten their health. Does this make food bad? The judgment of the black hat is an essential part of thinking, but some people overuse the black hat. This does not make the black hat a bad hat. In the same way the overuse of routines may be a bad thing, but this does not mean that routines as such are bad.

CHAPTER 7

Navy Formal Shoes

Freedom of Routines

In some ways routines provide freedom. If we had to think about every action we take, then life would be very slow and very complicated. Following a routine actually frees us to attend to matters that really need our attention.

The brain sets up routine patterns so that we can deal effectively with the world. That is the nature of perception. Instead of having to analyze each new experience, we simply recognize the situation by using a perceptual pattern. From time to time we need to challenge these perceptions and that is what we call creativity, but most of the time having these routine perceptions makes life possible.

Some people feel that all routines and structures are restricting. They want to be free of structures and to use their own initiative. For these people even the framework of the six hats and the six action shoes and the deliberate technique of lateral thinking are restrictive. They don't realize the difference between restricting structures and liberating structures:

- A railway line is restrictive in the sense that the train can run only along the track. At the same time the smoothness of the track allows an efficient use of energy.

- A locked room is a restrictive structure but also may free us from other cares so that we have time to think.

- A ladder is a liberating structure because it allows us to reach places we couldn't reach without it.

- A cup is a liberating structure because it allows us to drink more conveniently and more effectively.

- Mathematical notation is a liberating structure because it allows us to do operations we could not otherwise do. The same applies to musical notation.

The six hat framework, the six shoe framework, and the deliberate techniques of lateral thinking are liberating structures because they allow us to do things that would otherwise be difficult or even impossible.

With what should a surgeon operate if not with a scalpel or other tool?

We need to keep a balanced view of structures and routines. We should not overlook their value just because abuses of routine can be restrictive.

CHAPTER 8

Navy Formal Shoes

Source of Routines

Routines may gradually evolve and accumulate over time. The traditions and routines of a wedding are set down by custom. The routines of good manners have evolved over centuries. The routines associated with a craft also may have evolved over a long time and through a lot of experience. Routines that have evolved over time can be used but also can be challenged. The craft of painting furniture may have evolved routines to cope with slow-drying paint, but with today's fast-drying paint the routines can be changed. We sometimes are tempted to keep routines only for tradition's sake.

Some routines are set up by organizations just like laws are set up by society. These routines help people avoid errors, allow interaction between people, and represent crystallization of the best way of doing something. Such routines can be improved or even dropped, but at times we want and need to use them.

Then there are routines that individuals set up for themselves (like my routine of checking hotel drawers). They can have a high use if they simplify life. Instead of working things out each time, just switch into the routine—navy shoe action mode.

Navy Formal Shoes

What Should Routines Be Like?

- Routines should cover many situations.

- It should be easy to recognize when a particular routine needs to be used.

- Applying a routine should be straightforward. The steps should be clear and follow one another.

- The routine should be robust—that is, the purpose of the routine is achieved even if the steps are not carried out exactly as prescribed.

- Routines should be flexible enough to cope with special circumstances.

- Routines should be easy to learn and remember.

- Routines should make sense to those who use them. Their logic and value should be apparent.

- Routines must avoid doubt and confusion.

Designing routines takes skill. A routine should always be a little bit artificial, for example, because if it is too natural, then it is easy to forget that it is a routine.

CHAPTER 10

Navy Formal Shoes

The Use of Routines

Some basic questions can be asked about routines:

"Which routine should be used here?"

"What are the steps of this routine?"

"Is it necessary to combine routines?"

"Is some flexibility necessary?"

"Where can the flexibility be used?"

"Can this routine be improved?"

"Can I check the application of this routine?"

"What output or result do I expect?"

Just as learning the drill of mathematics helps simplify carrying out mathematical routines, the better a routine is known, the less trouble there is in using that routine.

I have spent some time making the case for routines because we take their value for granted and tend to focus only on their restrictive and negative aspects.

CHAPTER 11

Navy Formal Shoes

*Navy Shoe Action Mode
and Exercises*

"This is a navy shoe situation. We just have to go through the procedure step by step, no matter how boring. Don't try to be clever. Don't try to take short cuts, or we'll leave out something."

"Successful grant applications always depend on good navy shoe action. The value of the project is less important than the formality with which the application is made."

"There are times in mountaineering when navy action mode can save your life and the lives of your companions. Stick to routines that have been tried and tested. If you want to try out new ideas, then do so under easy conditions."

"If you had used some navy action formality on taking that case history, you would have saved him and us a lot of trouble. His father was a Native American Indian, and they do not grow facial hair. Because of that error we have spent time and money on complex hormone tests that were quite unnecessary."

"Some people are brilliant and can go straight to the fault. One day you may be like that. For the moment it is better to use the navy action mode and to follow the fault-checking routine. Inspiration is not enough."

"I would really like to set up a navy shoe routine here. We are getting too many errors."

"Make it simpler by using navy shoe action. Set up a routine, and then use it."

Navy shoe action mode requires the carrying through of established routines. The action focus is on choosing the appropriate routine and then carrying it through meticulously. Focus on the step that is being taken and think of the following step. Keep checking that the routine is being done properly.

The navy shoe action mode also can include establishing formal routines where these would have a value.

Exercises

Consider how the navy shoe action mode would be of value in each of the following situations. Why would this type of action have an advantage?

❶ Training an athlete

❷ Rearing a child

❸ Working as a newspaper reporter

❹ Managing a toy factory

❺ Working in an advertising agency

❻ Performing surgery

❼ Administering a school

❽ Working as a sales assistant in a store

CHAPTER 12

Navy Formal Shoes

Navy Shoe Action Style

Precisely using formal routines. Adhering to formality and procedure. Taking the laid down steps one after the other. Acknowledging that the routine has a value and purpose. Instead of going through the routine mindlessly just because you have to, there is a sense that the routine is the best action plan of the moment and that this action plan is being followed. You may ask a person to switch into the navy shoe action mode. People may decide for themselves that the situation demands the navy shoe action mode. In the framework of the six styles of action the navy shoe action mode has its rightful place. Quite often the best action is routine action. Sometimes routine action is absolutely necessary. Just as you would wish to carry out a dance routine effectively or to sing in tune, so you might desire to carry out a routine perfectly.

CHAPTER 13

Navy Formal Shoes

Summary

The navy formal shoe mode is one of the six action modes. It emphasizes formality and routines, such as the drills and routines of the navy. At times routines are essential to ensure safety and avoid error. Routines can represent a crystallization of the best way of doing something. Using routines can free up our thinking so that we can tackle other matters, but their overuse can stifle initiative and restrict flexibility. This does not make routines a bad thing but cautions against excessive use of what is a good thing.

A routine is an action pattern that has been laid down in advance. Once the appropriate routine has been selected, then action consists in fully carrying through this routine. 👣

PART IV
Grey Sneakers

"WE NEED TO KNOW WHY THERE HAS BEEN
this increase in absenteeism. Before we take any
other type of action we need some grey sneaker
action. Let's get more information."

"We are investigating it. We are still in grey
action mode. We'll let you know as soon as we
have anything."

"Just find out all you can. Limit yourself to grey
sneaker mode. Be as inconspicuous as possible.
Remember just the grey mode. No heroics."

Sneakers are quiet, and you can pad around in
them without being noticed. In a sense, in grey shoe
action mode the person is sneaking around, listening,
and exploring. The style is casual, relaxed, and quiet.
There is no desire to be noticed or even to affect other
people.

In a grey mist and fog you cannot see clearly to
find your way around. All your energy is directed at
getting information from the surroundings. In the
same way grey action mode implies removing the fog
of ignorance. We want to obtain as much information
as possible.

Grey also suggests the grey matter of the brain, as
in the colloquial, "Use your grey matter." So the grey
action mode includes both collecting information and
also thinking. When in the grey action mode, a person
may use any aids to thinking that he or she wishes,
such as the six thinking hats.

In the navy action mode you know exactly the
next step that has to be taken because you are following a known routine. In the grey action mode you are
exploring, but you do not know what you are going to
find. What you find determines your next step. If a

clue turns up, then you follow that clue. In the navy action mode you are reciting a poem you know by heart. In the grey action mode you are conducting a conversation that may turn in any direction.

Note that the grey action mode includes all the activities that are necessary in order to obtain the information. If the information is in a particular library, then tracking it down is part of the grey sneaker action mode. It is not just a sit-and-think mode.

Scientists pursuing a theory, investigating journalists, detectives solving a crime, market researchers trying to assess response to a new product, pollsters, investment bankers contemplating a takeover, and tax inspectors are all using the grey action mode. Perhaps the purest case of grey action mode would be the investigation of a computer fraud.

Sir Arthur Conan Doyle's famous detective, Sherlock Holmes, mainly involved himself in grey sneaker action. In the end the criminal usually confessed, thereby removing the need for more vigorous action. Today's television dramas allow less room for grey action mode and tend to emphasize orange and brown action modes.

The grey action mode can interplay with other action modes as information gathered reveals the need for other types of action. Quite often there may be a pause in other types of action until you get the information that you need to go forward. As with all the other action modes there is often an overlap of needs, and an action rarely consists of only one action mode.

CHAPTER 14

Grey Sneakers

The Use of Investigation

- *You need to investigate when you have no idea as to what is going on.* You're fishing. You're looking for leads. You want some basis on which to build a hypothesis. A scientist, an archaeologist, a searcher for oil, and a detective are often in this sort of position. There is a leak of sensitive information from a government department. Where do you start looking? When a patient first visits a doctor, the doctor has to search for clues. The doctor may indeed use some fixed routine for eliciting information—a combination of navy and grey shoe action. When a doctor forms an idea, then this hypothesis can be checked out by means of tests. So the first use of investigation is to make a start.

- *The mind can see only what it is prepared to see.* That is why a hypothesis is so useful. Using the framework of the hypothesis you can start to notice things you would not otherwise have noticed. The hypothesis also provides a direction in which to look for further information. The second use of information therefore is to confirm or reject hypotheses. In theory scientists should seek to destroy an hypothesis, but they first need something to destroy, so they attempt to confirm the hypothesis as theory. This second use of investigation is the checking-out phase.

- *Choices often have to be made.* You may need to choose between two possible hypotheses or two courses of action. You need information to make choices of any sort. A person buying a new stove wants to get as much information as possible, not only from the vendor but from existing users of that brand of stove.

- *You need information to build a case.* A prosecutor wants the detective to provide enough information to get a conviction. The designer of a new product wants as much information as possible about how the product will be perceived by the designated market. The information may not reach the level of certainty of proof, but the information must build a reasonable case.

- *You need information when looking into the future.* You need to see the consequences of action—and also of inaction. Today ecologists and green groups paint horrific scenarios about the green-house and other effects. You need information to assess the seriousness of the danger. Information about future possibilities gives a good basis for action.

- *Sometimes you need to know what you don't know.* You need to identify exactly what you don't know.

CHAPTER 15

Grey Sneakers

Thinking, Ideas, and Information

Thinking is involved in collecting information and making the maximum use of that information. Information may trigger ideas, which may trigger an information search. Information does not easily yield up all the ideas that are present in that information. The mind has to put things together in different ways—to generate possibilities and even provocations. Sometimes there is information which everyone has looked at in a particular way. Then someone comes along and uses lateral thinking to look at information in a different way and reaches a new hypothesis about it.

It is a mistake to believe that collecting enough information will do all our thinking for us. Information is not a substitute for ideas and thinking. On the other hand, there is a real need for information. The key is to sustain an active interplay between thinking and information collecting. Thinking directs information collecting and also makes the best use of what has been collected. At the same time information may suggest ideas, confirm some ideas, and lead to the rejection of others.

CHAPTER 16

Grey Sneakers

Use of the Grey Sneaker Action Mode

"Right now we are all in the grey sneaker action mode. We have to find out what our competitors are planning to do. That has to come first."

"Why are you trying to solve the problem in that way? Have you given it some grey action mode, or are you just doing the first thing that comes to mind?"

"We have only got half a story here. Get out there, put on your grey sneakers, and get the other half. Then we can publish it."

"How much is it all going to cost? Have you completed your grey actions on this?"

"He is always jumping to conclusions. He never checks things out. I don't think he likes the grey action mode. Perhaps it is too quiet for him. He prefers strong action."

"I congratulate you. That's very good grey sneaker action. That was a smart piece of investigation. It is going to save us a lot of time and money."

"How is it that those two scientists could show the effect but no one else has been able to? What is going on? Did they cheat? Did they make an honest mistake? Did they just do things in a

different way? There is a great need for some grey
sneaker action.''

10:42 P.M. U.K. TIME: TIME FOR SLEEP BEFORE ARRIVING IN LOS
ANGELES. STILL SUNNY AS WE TRAVEL WITH THE SUN.

CHAPTER 17

Grey Sneakers

Motivation for Grey Sneaker Action

1:50 A.M. U.K. TIME AND 5:50 P.M. LOS ANGELES TIME: AWAKE AFTER A BRIEF SLEEP.

What is the motivation for investigation and exploration? Investigation may be a large part of your job as a scientist, detective, explorer, or spy. Even so, some people satisfy the minimal requirements of such jobs, and some actually enjoy exploration. Some people have a natural curiosity and a fascination with information. They want to know things. Other people may not have this curiosity but instead have an urgency to complete a task once the task has been started. Such people may be slow to start grey sneaker action, but once started they are carried along by the momentum of what they are discovering. Like the proverbial terrier, they cannot let go.

Other people want only certainties. They are irritated by ambiguities and uncertainties. They want everything to be neat and defined. Such people are apt to switch into certainties and beliefs as soon as possible. They quickly become dogmatic and move rapidly from possibility to certainty without any proper justification.

What is a belief? A belief is an idea, a hypothesis, a theory, or a way of looking at the world which forces us to look at the world in a way that supports that belief. The classic example is paranoia. Paranoid people use complicated logic to show that all events are directed toward themselves. Unlike some other types of mental illness in paranoia there is no lack of organization of information but a type of excess of organization. Everything is fitted together into one master theory.

In an investigation this type of person rushes to generate an idea or hypothesis. All further investigation is designed to fit that hypothesis, which soon becomes a belief—which must be true. Anything that does not fit is ignored or changed so that it does fit. Objective exploration ceases. As a lawyer in court makes and argues a particular case, so does the investigator. This is dangerous grey shoe action. The best preventative for this premature closing of the mind is to insist that in grey shoe action at least two hypotheses are kept in mind and that the investigator should be able to make a reasonable case for both of them at any time.

The premature acceptance of a theory also causes trouble in science. An early reasonable hypothesis causes scientists to look at the world in a particular way and then ignore evidence that does not fit the hypothesis. All evidence is seen through this hypothesis. It can take a long time for a breakthrough to break through even though the evidence was there all along.

CHAPTER 18

Grey Sneakers

What Should Investigation Be Like?

A formal collection of information can take the form of house-to-house inquiries in a murder hunt. A scientist tests many possible variations of a chemical molecule. A pollster defines a sample and steadily works through it. This is navy type action used for grey purposes.

OVER THE MIDWEST AT 39,000 FEET AND TRAVELING AT 926 KILOMETERS PER HOUR. ONE HOUR AND FIFTY-FOUR MINUTES TO ARRIVAL IN LOS ANGELES.

The data should be neutral and objective even though eventually they are looked at through the window of an idea. Having more than one person involved in collecting the data reduces the personal bias of an individual. This type of data collection is driven by a systematic method.

The other type of data collection is driven by a hunch or theory that hypothesizes what data to look for and where to find it. It requires a conscious effort by the grey sneaker operator to make a clear distinction between a theory that helps data collection and data collection that simply supports the theory. There may be a need for a second person to show that the same data can indeed be looked at in a different way. There can also be the habit, suggested earlier, of always having at least two theories or hypotheses in mind.

There is no easy way around the dilemma that without a theory it may be difficult even to collect data but that the theory may so dominate the data collection that it is no longer neutral or comprehensive. Instead of pretending that people can be objective it may be better to acknowledge that the mind cannot really be objective and then to take steps to address that lack of objectivity (like the habit of twin hypotheses).

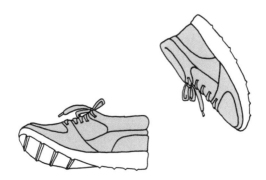

C H A P T E R 1 9

Grey Sneakers

Investigation Leads to Action

Navy shoe formality may be involved in collecting data, and that may lead to grey shoe activity. This in turn may lead to brown shoe (or other) action.

Investigation itself is a form of action, but at some point grey shoe action gives way to other forms of action and activity. A scientist moves from data to theory to experiment to data to publication of a paper. A detective collects evidence to build a case, which is passed to the prosecutor, who then presents the case in court. In between comes the arrest of the person to be charged. A market researcher takes action to collect information, which is then passed to the client, who decides what action to take. An interplay occurs between the collection of information and the action that is going to be taken as a result of that information. The key question for the grey shoe operator to ask is, "At this moment what is the central purpose of my activity—to collect information?" If the answer to that question is yes, then grey sneaker action is called for.

The movement from information collection to action depends on several factors: What is the time pressure? Is there a hurry? Will delay have negative consequences? What are the dangers of precipitate action? What are the benefits of quick action? What is the trade-off between more thorough data collection and the need for action? If a criminal suspect is preparing to flee the country, further collection of evidence may make a better case, but there would be no suspect to try. In some cases spending twice as much money and time in collecting data produces a benefit that is only 10 percent better. That may not be a worthwhile investment if the information is for a market survey. In other fields the extra information might be vital: in medicine one additional test may make the difference between recommending and not recommending a procedure.

Some ways of collecting information are more effective than others. One way may take a long time and cost a great deal of money; another way make be quicker and cheaper. The collection of data is an activity like any other and can be improved through careful and creative thinking. It is not often that data must be collected regardless of cost. Information is a product like any other. What is the best way of producing that product? The careful design of data collection is as important as the use of the data.

CHAPTER 20

Grey Sneakers

*Carrying Through Grey
Sneaker Action and Exercises*

The data collector must be absolutely clear that at the moment he or she is in grey sneaker mode. Information collection requires full concentration and must take precedence over other matters. The casual and incidental collection of information does have a high value, but with grey sneaker mode the purpose of the action is direct collection of information. Collecting the information is an end in itself. Grey sneaker action requires effort and discipline. It is easy to slip into other action modes that offer a reaction to the situation and make use of existing action habits. Grey sneaker action is quiet and unobtrusive. If the data collector uses an authority role (purple boot action mode), then the data provider might tell the collector only what is expected.

The information collector should be almost invisible. That is why the color grey is so appropriate—a grey cat is always difficult to see.

Persistence is probably the most important characteristic needed for the grey sneaker mode. If you do have persistence, then a lot else will follow. If you do not have persistence, then all other qualities will amount to nothing.

2:40 A.M. U.K. TIME: STOP FOR SNACK AS WE APPROACH LOS ANGELES.

56

Exercises

Describe the grey sneaker action component in each of the following situations. Where and how is grey sneaker action required?

❶ Working on an assembly line

❷ Running for reelection

❸ Marrying someone you have know for three months

❹ Suddenly rising juvenile crime in an area

❺ Driving along a highway to a destination that is 200 miles distant

❻ Interviewing someone for a job

❼ Deciding in what color to decorate a room

❽ Buying a computer

CHAPTER 21

Grey Sneakers

Grey Sneaker Action Style

Information collection as a priority. Quiet, unobtrusive, and objective. Collecting information as a basis for theories and then collecting information to test the theories. Asking, looking, and listening. Designing ways of collecting the information. Collecting information most effectively. Being conscious of the value of an hypothesis and also of the danger of an hypothesis, which can reduce objectivity.

Grey sneaker action style also includes thinking. The formal application of thinking to a chosen target area. The solution of problems. Making the maximum use of available information and deciding what further information may be required.

In general, grey sneaker action mode is absorbing information and using it. Action is required to collect information, and skill is involved in deciding how to collect the information, in collecting the information, and in making the best use of it.

CHAPTER 22

Grey Sneakers

Summary

The grey sneaker action mode is one of the six action modes. It emphasizes the collection and use of information. Think of grey as indicating the grey matter of the brain because it is brain rather than muscle that is important in grey sneaker mode. Think also of a grey fog or mist because the purpose of grey sneaker action is to remove the fog to make things clear. The sneaker type of shoe suggests something that is casual, quiet, and unobtrusive.

In the grey sneaker mode the objectives are the collection and use of information. They must take precedence over everything else. Information may be collected systematically where this is possible, but other times a theory or hypothesis may be needed to suggest a direction. Remember that the collection of information should be as comprehensive and neutral as possible. It is only in the second phase that information collection may be directed at testing a hypothesis.

Information collecting is a valuable activity that is the basis for many other types of action. 👣

PART V
Brown Brogues

"THIS IS BROWN BROGUE STUFF. GET IN THERE and see what you can do. Be sensible, be practical. Work it out as you go along."

"I'm operating in the brown brogue mode. Each step is determined by the evolving situation. I have a general sense of direction, but the choice of action at any moment is purely practical."

"There is no fixed price. You just bargain. It is a sort of brown brogue way of conducting business. He sets the price flexibly, and you pay flexibly."

"You want to be told what to do. Well, I'll tell you. Use the brown brogue action mode. Do what is sensible and practical at every moment."

Brown is a practical color. The earth is brown, and mud is brown. There is nothing exotic about the color brown, which is basic and indeed earthy. Brown is an everyday color. Brogues are stout shoes capable of hard wear; they are not smart shoes for formal occasions but day-to-day shoes for most occasions. All these factors contribute to what is meant by the brown brogue action mode.

The emphasis in brown brogue action is on practicality, pragmatism, and good sense. What can be done in this situation? Navy shoe action is determined by a preset routine that has to be followed. Brown brogue action is determined moment to moment by the actual situation. Quite often the situation falls outside established routine or training.

Flexibility is a key aspect of brown brogue action. You change your behavior as the situation changes. If you cannot do what you set out to do, you modify your objective. There is no rigidity about brown brogue action. You do what can be done. You do what you can do.

Brown brogue action is low key and unspectacular. There is something to be done, and you do it. Good sense, common sense, and a little wisdom are required. General experience can be a help, but general experience may have set up bad habits of behavior that interfere with the true flexibility required for brown brogue action. Experience can trap people in routines of perception and behavior and lead to navy shoe behavior. But experience also can help to prevent overreaction and provide a sense of perspective. Experience can provide a sort of calmness in coping.

Brown brogue action is not detached and advisory but is always involved: it is "get your hands dirty" action. Without thinking there would only be mindless action, but the thinking is directed to what can be done in the moment.

What are sometimes called street smarts come under brown brogue action. The general skills of doing—for which I invented the word *operacy*—are best illustrated by brown brogue action. Schools teach about literacy and numeracy, but in the real world operacy is just as important. Knowledge does not automatically lead to action. Matters like assessing priorities and guessing well are important parts of life, of operacy, and of brown brogue action.

When I fly short distances, I ask for a window seat because I enjoy looking at the world outside. When I fly long distances, I prefer an aisle seat because it makes it easier to reach the lavatory in the middle of the night. That is a sort of brown brogue action— although you could argue that the window person climbing over me might wake me up. On balance, it seems to make sense to me.

I have often suggested that airport information desks should have simple overhead projectors providing instant information that could be updated as often as required. Passengers then would know when and why delays occurred instead of crowding around desks to hear announcements. I have been told that the idea is too simple and that the airlines are developing a complicated electronic screen—which probably will be out of order half the time. Simplicity and practicality are key features of brown brogue action.

The small cartons of fruit juice have been a huge success. The fruit juice is the same, but the handy size and the attached straw provide great convenience. Brown brogue action is concerned with what is doable and what gives value.

This book is being written entirely on a flight from London to Auckland, New Zealand, where I have been invited to address the meeting of the Commonwealth Law Society. Why? Because writing a book is by far the best way to make the time pass quickly. Because it is a period of total peace when I am not going to be interrupted by phone calls or other matters. Because there is nothing else that I could, or should, be doing. Because being 35,000 feet up does give one a certain detachment. Because I have found it better to write books like this in one go rather than a piece at a time. Because I wrote another book, *Six Thinking Hats*, on a plane trip from London to Melbourne. On that occasion I used a Canon 5 Star electronic typewriter, which meant messing around with pieces of paper. This time I'm using a small Psion MC400 mobile computer, which removes the need for paper and also is quieter.

Brown brogue action may also include twisting your tie back to front when eating on a plane so that dropped food does not ruin the tie. These are minor points of practicality.

Brown brogue action is not heroics but small practical things that come together to give effectiveness.

CHAPTER 23

Brown Brogues

Pragmatism

Some people condemn pragmatism because they believe that pragmatism seems to be a way of acting without principles. Pragmatism does not mean being unprincipled: it means the pragmatic use of principles. Pragmatism is when you do what can be done to achieve an objective and put as much emphasis on practicality as on principles. Action without principles is dangerous and intolerable in a civilized society because principles help society control action.

The main objection to pragmatism is that the end might come to justify the means. If offering false evidence to convict a drug dealer is acceptable because the end is worthwhile, then the door is opened to all sorts of behavior. Pragmatism, however, asserts that the end cannot justify the means without leading to total chaos. Much theft, for example, would be justified on the grounds of need.

Pragmatism is concerned with where an action might lead—with the effect or consequences of the action—but it does not say that anything is acceptable as long as the outcome is positive. Pragmatism should be contrasted with the arrogance (often based on principles) that declares, ''I am sure that what I am doing is right, and I do not care what the consequences might be.''

Pragmatism means being sensitive to a situation, to the people involved in the situation, and to what is practical. Pragmatism is the art of the possible. Politicians are pragmatic people.

The term *expediency* also has a bad image. Politicians are said to do things in order to gain votes even though these things may be unprincipled. Buying votes with favors is an unpleasant practice, and some types of expediency are not acceptable. Nevertheless, it may not be hygienic to use a dirty handkerchief to staunch a flow of blood, but if there is nothing else on hand then one urgent need overrides the danger. An infection can be dealt with later.

CHAPTER 24

Brown Brogues

Effectiveness

In the course of my work I have met a lot of highly intelligent and creative people. But what seems to be more rare than intelligence or creativity is simple effectiveness. Effectiveness is very much a part of brown brogue action. Brown brogue action is not just concerned with survival and getting by, even though that may sometimes be the priority. Brown brogue action is concerned with getting results.

Efficiency and effectiveness are not at all the same thing. Efficiency is a balance between input and output. There is an effort to cut down on input and costs so that the ratio looks good. Effectiveness means making sure that the resources are available to get the results that you want. If the resources are not sufficient to allow you to do everything that you need to do, then you list priorities and go down that list as far as you can. But you make sure that each item you tackle is done effectively. Effectiveness does not mean inefficiency. It means focusing directly on what you want to achieve rather than on the balance between input and output. An efficient operation may give a poor quality output. To some extent the Japanese tend to put effectiveness first, whereas the Americans tend to put efficiency first: the Americans removed all extras from cars to decrease the price, and the Japanese put in as many extras as possible to increase the value.

It is a good habit to ask at every step, what is the most effective course of action here? That is a good brown brogue habit.

4:30 A.M. U.K. TIME, 8:30 P.M. LOS ANGELES TIME: LANDING AT LOS ANGELES AIRPORT. SITTING IN THE TRANSIT LOUNGE.

CHAPTER 25

Brown Brogues

What Is the Basis of Brown Brogue Action?

Brown brogue action is a combination of good values, good sense, and good principles.

What are good values? Human respect is an example of a good value. From this basic value comes an avoidance of bullying, pressure, extortion, torture, prejudice, racism, etc. Human respect is a practical aspect of the love that religions advocate. You can respect an enemy even when you feel you can't love that enemy. Respect acknowledges others' dignity and right to exist. Being unwilling to cause harm is another basic value. One of the most basic values in medicine is not to cause more harm than help: sometimes the side effects of drugs do just that. Respect for the truth is another basic value and so is respect for the environment.

There are individual values, community values, social values, and environmental values. Unless the brown brogue action is specifically directed toward doing something directly in these areas, the minimum requirement is to avoid doing harm. If a person is in good standing in a community, then to destroy that standing unreasonably is causing harm to the community. To arrest a person as publicly as possible causes such harm. An arrested person is not yet a convicted person (that is for the courts to decide), so there is no justification for this harm.

Should brown brogue action attempt to create benefits or positive values as such? Probably not, unless this is the specific purpose of the action. A slight additional effort may be able to create such additional values, but it is usually difficult enough to achieve the main objective of the brown brogue action, and blurring one objective with another may confuse the action and make it less effective.

What is good sense? In hindsight, everything that works out well can be attributed to common sense and any failure to lack of common sense. Good sense and common sense are most easily visible in hindsight when everything has been worked out. It is not unlike standing beside a roulette table when the number twenty-three comes up. If you had had the good sense to put your money on number twenty-three, then you would have won a lot of money. Hindsight is easy. So a plea for common sense is usually pointless. Good sense is a combination of sensitivity, priorities, and practicality. Sensitivity means clear understanding of the situation and of the people involved. This is a matter of perception and also of trying out different perceptions. This sensitivity does not mean sympathy or compassion but an understanding of what is going on. Establishing priorities is very much part of brown brogue action. Without a good sense of priorities it is difficult to lay down the necessary action steps. Priorities set objectives and guidelines for action. What do you want to achieve? What matters most? What needs to be done first?

The final component of good sense is practicality. This is an acknowledgment of what is actually doable. You might like to do some things, but they may not be feasible. What can actually be done? This should not give rise to a sense of timidity and the setting of timid objectives. The sense of practicality extends to a feeling of what is likely. What is likely to happen? How is the situation likely to evolve? What is the likely reaction to an intervention? To some extent this assessment of what is likely depends on experience and understanding human nature. But even a simple pause to ask, "What is the most likely outcome here?" can make a significant difference. It is important to distinguish between the likely and the possible. There are times when the possible does indeed happen, but in general you are going to be better off aiming for the likely.

What are good principles? That the end cannot justify the means is a basic principle. A concern for the truth is both a principle and a value. There are general moral principles such as these and also practical principles of action. The latter might include the need to define your role, your resources, and your objectives. Another practical principle is to define the action mode that you want to use. Is it really brown action mode, or might it be a purple action mode? Being reliable when others have to depend on you is a further important principle.

These guidelines for behavior in the brown brogue action mode may seem much like the guidelines for training the perfect person who acts appropriately on every occasion. This is true but refers to only one of the six action modes. The pragmatic nature of brown brogue action requires a double sensitivity:

1. A sensitivity to the situation.

2. A sensitivity to guiding principles.

This is the definition of pragmatic behavior. The other five action modes do not have this characteristic.

CHAPTER 26

Brown Brogues

Initiative

Since there are no formal rules of procedure, then a person in the brown brogue action mode needs to use initiative. Analyze the situation and determine priorities and objectives. Behave in the most obvious and established way. This depends on a personal repertoire of action steps provided by experience. If the action does not work, then try another approach. Always do the obvious thing first unless you are sure that surprise is important. There may be a place for creativity if the value of a creative approach is high and the cost of failure low. Is this the right situation in which to risk a new and untried approach?

Patterns of action depend on individual personalities and styles. The extrovert may behave in a way that is different from the introvert. No one pattern is right for everyone. That is the difference between the navy action mode and the brown action mode. With the navy action mode there is one routine that has to be used by everyone. Brown action mode is more customized and more individualized.

Because brown action mode is individual, there is training value in discussing what has been done in debriefing sessions. Why did you do that? What did you do next? In sales training colleagues quickly learn from the behavior of a master salesperson because there is a tangible measure of success (the sales volume). This instant measurement of success is more difficult to find in other fields. So training should include an acknowledgment of the success of the action. This acknowledgment may be based on many criteria—effectiveness, speed, simplicity, low cost, low risk. All these aspects need to be discussed.

Brown action mode does not mean having to create an action pattern from scratch on each occasion. When you get up in the morning, you have a choice of clothes to wear (as distinct from having to wear a uniform). So the brown action operator may choose from a range of available action patterns. But the choice is up to the operator.

CHAPTER 27

Brown Brogues

Use of the Brown Brogue Action Mode

"There is no set way of doing this. Keep your head. Be practical. Use the brown brogue mode. Make your decisions as you go along."

"He's fine in routine situations. A great navy action person. But not so good at the brown brogue stuff. He does not seem to have any common sense."

"We are going to put the books aside and use the brown brogue mode. You know, practical and moment-to-moment action depending on what we find. We have our objectives and our priorities for guides."

"I liked the way you used your initiative. That was a very good example of brown brogue action mode. You are getting pretty good at it."

"What do we do now? I don't yet know. We'll wait and see how the situation develops and then decide what to do. Brown brogue stuff."

"I am sorry I just froze up. I couldn't think of a thing to do. I guess I am not very good at this brown brogue action mode."

"Yes, that is a reasonable plan of action. You can try it, but if you find it does not work then switch to the brown brogue action mode."

"There are times when doing nothing at all is the correct brown brogue action mode."

"She is totally the wrong sort of person for that job. She has no feel for situations. She does not understand what is meant by pragmatism. She wants to do everything by the book. But the book does not cover all situations. She just does not seem happy with brown brogue action."

CHAPTER 28

Brown Brogues

Source of Brown Brogue Action

Brown brogue action is determined in the first place by the needs of the situation. What are you there for? What are you trying to do? What sort of situation is it? Brown brogue action is, above all, responsive to the situation.

Brown brogue action follows a simple analysis, understanding, or appreciation of the situation. What is going on? How is it likely to develop? What are the sensitive points in the situation? What are the action points? What are the needs?

Brown brogue action requires simple initiatives. Keep things as simple as possible. Do the obvious—except in a conflict situation where surprise may have a benefit. Don't try to be clever. Prefer to be practical.

Brown brogue action draws on your experience and also the experience of others. What action patterns are available to you? What did you do in the past in similar situations?

Although brown brogue action is responsive to the situation, always try to be in control of the situation. Avoid letting the situation get out of control so that you are carried along and have to respond to the initiatives of others.

CHAPTER 29

Brown Brogues

What Should Brown Brogue Action Be Like? and Exercises

Brown brogue action should be simple, practical, and effective. There is nothing more to be said. Everything is covered in those three words.

Use them to test any brown brogue actions:

- Are the actions simple enough?

- Are the actions practical (doable)?

- Are the actions likely to be effective?

If the answers to these three questions are not an easy yes, then think again. Brown brogue action is not mindless action. It includes the thinking necessary to choose suitable actions.

Exercises

For each of the following situations suggest a brown brogue course of action.

❶ A father asks your advice because he suspects his son is a thief.

❷ You are waiting patiently in a line when some newcomers move directly to the head of the line.

❸ You are in a public meeting that is constantly interrupted by someone with a grievance who makes the same point over and over again.

❹ You are in a store and notice that the man in front of you is stealing some of the merchandise.

❺ At a party one of the guests gets drunk and wants to pick a fight with you.

5:54 A.M. U.K. TIME, 9:54 P.M. LOS ANGELES TIME: RETURN TO PLANE TE001.

❻ A neighbor always parks her car so that it blocks the entrance to your garage. When you come back late at night, you are unable to get into your garage.

❼ Someone unknown is spreading false rumors that your business is in difficulties and is likely to go bankrupt.

❽ You are driving a distance of fifty miles to get to an important meeting for which you cannot be late. After twenty miles you hear a strange sound coming from the back of the car. What do you do?

Brown Brogues

Brown Brogue Action Style

The style is low key and practical. You don't go in with any set plan, but you assess the situation moment to moment and act accordingly. The emphasis is on practicality and effectiveness. You do what is doable. There is a need for a clear sense of objectives and a clear sense of priorities. Within these guidelines you determine your actions. Take initiatives and don't be passive. Keep control of the situation. Be sensitive to changes in the situation. Give yourself space for action and fallback positions in case things do not work out as intended. Have plans, but don't be trapped by them. Be flexible: if the situation changes, then adjust to that change. Keep your head and use it. Pragmatism is the key aspect of brown brogue action.

CHAPTER 31

Brown Brogues

Summary

Think of brown earth and down to earth. Think of mud and messy situations. Think of the practicality of brogues, which are hard-wearing shoes suitable for most occasions. The result is brown brogue action mode that is low key and practical. Assess the situation, and then act on your own initiative. Your actions will be guided by basic values, principles, good sense, and a feel for what is possible. The emphasis is always on simplicity, practicality, and effectiveness. Over time you will build up basic action patterns: pick and choose from these as the situation requires. A strong sense of priorities and likelihood is useful in guiding your choice of action. Be pragmatic, and be flexible. Keep in control of the situation even as you adjust to it. In brown brogue mode you watch and you act.

PART VI

Orange Gumboots

"**I**T'S AN EMERGENCY. THE RIVER IS FLOODING. Orange gumboot action mode. Action."

"I know it is an orange gumboot situation, but we do have to think it out. Mindless action is no use."

"At any moment this scandal could blow up in our faces. It's orange gumboot action mode. We have to move very fast."

"We have now moved into an orange gumboot action mode. The situation has changed. The priorities have changed. Safety is now a priority. If property gets damaged, that's too bad."

Think of orange as a color for warnings and alarms because it is easily visible. Think of the rubber boots that fire fighters wear.

Gumboots are not normal wear. You wear them for special situations. Surgeons wear rubber boots or gumboots. Hunters sometimes wear them. Orange gumboots suggest special occasions.

Orange is not a gentle color: it is vivid and striking. The color shrieks. Alarm bells ring.

From both the color and the style of the gumboots we get the sense that orange gumboot action mode is directly concerned with emergency situations. Once something is classified as an emergency, then priorities change. There are new rules for action.

Everyone faces emergencies from time to time in the form of accidents, crime, or illness. For most people these are rare situations. For other people—police officers, fire fighters, doctors, paramedics, soldiers in action, construction workers—emergencies are a part of their daily lives. There are various other forms of crisis, as well—business crises due to financial problems or personnel problems (such as strikes) and domestic crises of various sorts. Severity, suddenness, and need for action are the characteristics of situations that demand orange gumboot action.

Any situation that threatens danger requires orange gumboot action. The danger may be to the people within the situation—in a fight or an attempted suicide. The danger may be to innocent people who are not responsible in any way for the situation—such as a flood or an accident involving a vehicle carrying toxic material. The danger may be to the people who are tackling problems—fire fighters in a forest blaze or police officers in a drug raid. Accidents of any sort usually require an orange gumboot response because speed is essential to save human lives and limit the damage.

In the United States about 50,000 lives a year might be saved if all cars proceeded at five miles per hour. There would then be few deaths from traffic accidents. Valuable as these 50,000 lives are, we don't restrict travel to five miles per hour because we feel it would be impractical. We accept a degree of risk in order for society to function effectively. We try to minimize risk, for example, by making cars safe and by penalizing drunk driving, but risks do remain, especially the natural disaster risks like flooding, earthquakes, and forest fires.

CHAPTER 32

Orange Gumboots

Characteristics of Emergency Situations

Are there some general characteristics of emergency situations that require orange gumboot action? Situations vary enormously, but we can try to identify some basic features.

- *A danger to human life or lives is present.* In emergencies human lives are at risk. These lives may belong to the people involved, to innocent bystanders, or to those who have to cope with the situation. Environmental emergencies, such as a major oil spill from a tanker like the *Exxon Valdez* in Alaska, can cause an immediate danger to human life or a long-term danger to the environment.

- *Events happen quickly.* The time frame in emergencies is usually much shorter than with other situations. Events may already have happened rapidly and may continue to develop in a rapid fashion.

- *The situation is unstable.* An unstable emergency situation can suddenly become much worse. A major volcanic eruption might be followed by a bigger eruption or none at all. Sometimes the response to a situation causes more harm that the original event. The panic following an earth tremor may cause more deaths than the tremor itself, or disease following a river flooding and contamination of the water supply may be worse than the flooding. Thus emergency situations can be explosive in the literal sense as well as in a system sense.

- *The situation is unpredictable.* Emergency situations involving people (hostages, mentally unstable people, suicides) are unpredictable because the people involved may be emotionally unstable and because the stress of the situation may make people act in an unpredictable manner. The instability of the situation and the rapid time frame also make prediction difficult. With natural disasters it is difficult to predict what will happen next. This unpredictability is not always present, however. With a major train crash the accident has happened and is not going to continue happening; the unpredictable factor is the medical condition of those involved.

- *Action of some sort is required urgently.* Action may be required to contain or remove the danger. This may be done by removing people from the danger zone or by removing the danger itself. Action may be required to warn people of danger, as in the contamination of a water supply. Action may be required to bring medical attention to those who have been injured. In general, the sooner injured people receive medical attention, the greater their chances of survival. In an emergency doing nothing is usually not an option. Even without an immediate danger public and political pressures may demand that something be done. If a person climbs to the top of a tall building and threatens to commit suicide by jumping, one response might be to keep people away from the base of the building. But society requires that some people should risk their lives to prevent the person from carrying out the suicide threat. So emergencies almost always demand action.

- *Someone usually can be blamed in an emergency.* Someone may be responsible for causing the emergency in the first place, or someone may be responsible for dealing with it. It is human nature to want to blame a disaster on someone.

7:16 A.M. U.K. TIME, 11:16 P.M. LOS ANGELES TIME: PLANE NOW AIRBORNE. FLYING TIME TO AUCKLAND IS 12 HOURS, 30 MINUTES.

- *When the emergency is over, some people claim that it could have been handled differently.* This is the great benefit of hindsight.

- *Standard reaction patterns are ineffective because each situation is unique.* As experience with hostage taking, fires, earthquakes, and so on, accumulates, however, an area of expertise can be drawn on and used. Experience with hostage taking, for example, has resulted in profiles of how those involved are likely to react and the best times for intervention. Such expertise will grow.

- *Emotions are heavily activated.* Dealing with the emotions of those who are directly involved and those who are involved through television and newspaper reports may be a major part of emergency action.

- *Impotence often characterizes the situation.* For a variety of reasons it often may be impossible to take the most obvious course of action. In some cases there is no available course of action.

Many of the above characteristics apply only to major emergencies. But minor emergencies are just as real as major emergencies. You are no more dead because a hundred other people around are also dead. Minor emergencies involving one or a few people are routine for police and fire departments but lack the extra pressures caused by media and political involvement.

The following major characteristics apply to all emergencies, including minor ones:

- Threat of danger or harm
- Rapid onset or quick acceleration of the situation
- Unstable situation
- Unpredictable development and outcome— or predictable harm
- Urgent action usually required
- No standard reaction patterns available
- Emotions heavily involved

Urgency and danger characterize an emergency situation. Insidious dangers with a slow buildup may not be treated as emergencies although they should. This applies to many environmental dangers.

CHAPTER 33

Orange Gumboots
Classification of the Situation

The spectrum of emergency situations ranges from those that are clearly orange mode in nature to others that have elements of orange mode. Many situations may be a mixture of orange and brown action modes. A situation also may suddenly change into orange mode if a human life is endangered.

Most organizations have ways of classifying and labeling major emergency situations, but expressions such as *red alert* apply only to major situations. Orange gumboot mode applies to a wider variety of situations because it describes not the situation but the action mode.

Once a situation is classified as requiring orange gumboot action, then the nature of the situation is set and the priorities are determined. The basic priority is to remove, contain, or minimize the danger. At this point other considerations are less important. The focus becomes clear. What is the existing danger? What are the potential dangers? How can the dangers be removed, contained, or minimized?

A road accident has happened. What are the dangers? One danger is more cars will pile up unless warning is given. Another danger is that those involved may suffer unless they get medical attention quickly.

CHAPTER 34

Orange Gumboots

Guidelines for Orange Mode Action

1. Assess the existing situation as accurately as possible. Determine what needs to be known and how it can be found out (for example, the nature of a toxic chemical that has spilled).

2. Assess the potential development of the situation in terms of what is likely and what is possible.

3. Assess the existing and potential dangers to the people directly involved, innocent bystanders, those who intervene, and the environment and property. Some people may wish to consider the political effects.

4. Determine who needs to be involved, who is in charge, and the lines of communication between the various parties involved. Set up methods of decision making and planning.

5. Avoid actions that might make things worse.

6. Decide on a strategy, but be prepared to change or modify the strategy if it is not working or if events demand a change. Avoid overreacting to every change and following events instead of taking the initiative.

7. You may need two parallel strategies. One strategy may minimize and contain the danger (evacu-

ating people in danger); the second strategy may tackle the cause of the danger directly, in cases where this is possible.

8. Develop and review a variety of action options. Some actions may not solve the crisis but may tilt the balance the right way. Some actions may put you in a better position if things move in a certain direction. Think ahead to deal with eventualities.

9. Reassess the situation periodically, even when nothing new has happened. Reassess whenever there is a development or change in circumstances.

10. Never panic or permit others to panic. Panic never improves the quality of the actions of those involved. People who do not fully appreciate the danger in which they have been placed must be informed—but without causing panic.

In certain circumstances another guideline must be followed:

11. Formulate a strategy for dealing with public announcements and the media. This requires direct attention and coordination among those involved.

At times waiting it out is the best strategy, as in hostage situations. People tire and moods change, so waiting it out instead of taking precipitate action may be the better choice. In most other situations waiting is not an option because the situation is likely to worsen. It is difficult to justify inaction when things do get worse. At the very beginning of a crisis a spontaneous reaction might avert the crisis, but once the crisis is established, there is probably no room for spontaneity.

Actions need to be designed, planned, and assessed. There is room for hunches and intuition, provided these do not increase the danger and provided there is a strong fallback position if the initiative fails.

8:06 A.M. U.K. TIME, 12:06 A.M. LOS ANGELES TIME: ANOTHER DINNER.

In conflict situations you may need to apply the techniques of negotiation. These involve perceptions, values, expectations, and power. Important parts of negotiation are establishing trust and communication and designing action options.

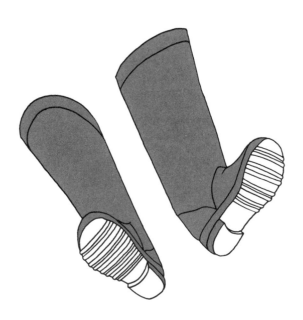

CHAPTER 35

Orange Gumboots

Courage

Orange action mode requires courage of all sorts. Physical courage is required to tackle an armed robber or to enter a burning building. Another type of courage is needed to make a decision and follow a strategy knowing that things may not work out as hoped. There is also the background courage of acting and knowing that the safety of others depends on your thinking and your actions.

Courage does not mean deliberately embracing risks, as in a Hollywood tough-guy movie: "I'm going in there." Courage involves minimizing and avoiding risks.

Entrepreneurs sometimes appear to be courageous risk-takers, but in interviewing entrepreneurs for a book on success I found that many hated risks and tried hard to have the odds stacked in their favor. Furthermore, what often appeared to be a risk to other people was not a risk at all for the entrepreneur who had investigated the matter thoroughly. At times entrepreneurs mistakenly believed they were not taking risks. The point is that such people do not set out to take risks; they set out to minimize risks.

CHAPTER 36

Orange Gumboots
Risk

The risks of any action need to be weighed against the risks of inaction. In some cases inaction is not very visible. In an emergency situation inaction is very visible as a form of action.

There are often three types of risk associated with action:

- The action will cause more harm and damage.

- It will fail to achieve its purpose.

- It will close off further options.

The big danger is that an action will make things worse. Where people are involved, the other party may panic with disastrous results. If an action can fail with no negative effects, no resetting of the situation, and no closing off of further options, then there is little risk in trying it. Fear of failure should not be a bar to action in such cases. So the key test is the question, "Will this make things worse if it does not succeed?"

CHAPTER 37

Orange Gumboots
Backup and Fallback Positions

Risk is reduced if a backup position is designed to be implemented should the initial operation falter. Sometimes this new and secure fallback position can be designed as a secondary objective: "If we don't reach the main objective, then we'll try for this secondary objective." In general, resources, thinking power, time, and initiative are on the side of the orange mode operator. These benefits should therefore be used carefully. Resources include access to expert opinion in fields such as psychology or chemistry.

Design is a key word. Design means bringing resources to the emergency in a systematic manner. Design is impeded when too many people are involved in decision making. Advice should be taken from many people, but designs and decisions are best left to one person or a small group. A good design is not a democratic consensus.

Every action taken should fit into the design. In the orange gumboot mode there is a greater need for strategy and design than in the brown brogue mode, which is more reactive.

If the disaster is major, then it is important to review the available concepts. What are these concepts? How can they be carried through? There may be a need for new concepts, for deliberate creative thinking—for some green hat thinking.

CHAPTER 38

Orange Gumboots

*What Should Orange Mode
Thinking Be Like?*

1. This is our assessment of the current situation.

2. These are the existing dangers, and these are the potential dangers that might develop.

3. These are the practical actions that can be taken right now to reduce (contain) the danger (to people, environment, property).

4. This is our overall strategy. We shall review it from time to time to see how it is working and how it fits changing circumstances.

5. We have obtained expert advice in the following matters.

6. We are working with the following groups, and the lines of communication are as follows.

7. These are the alternatives we have considered and the reasons we have put them aside for the moment.

8. We assess the risks as follows. We assess the chances of success as follows.

CHAPTER 39

Orange Gumboots
Design for Action

Orange mode actions need to be designed. The routine approach of the navy shoes cannot be applied. The free initiative of the brown brogues is not rigorous enough. There is a need to take grey sneaker action to collect information and then to move into orange mode and design a strategy.

Simply thinking of the ultimate objective is not enough. Every subobjective and every step toward the objectives must be designed. The means must be specified as well as the ends. Alternative steps have to be generated, considered, and assessed. The possible outcomes of each step must be examined. The priorities of the orange mode are very clear: minimize the danger. Everything is assessed against this priority.

As in chess steps may be taken to create a situation in which the final step will be effective. Every advantage is worth having, but it is not worth going for a short-term advantage if this has a long-term negative consequence.

Getting the situation under control is the first step. Until the situation is under control, action is going to be haphazard.

CHAPTER 40

Orange Gumboots

*Carrying Through
Orange Mode Action*

Carrying through orange mode action requires control, decisiveness, and a unified strategy. All those involved need to work as a team. Different opinions can be put forward up to the moment of a decision, but after that there should be cooperation. Modifications to moment-to-moment tactics can be suggested as long as the benefits are clearly stated. If such modifications are rejected, they stay rejected. Everyone needs to know exactly what is to be done and who is to do it. The backup, follow-through, and fallback actions—and the points at which they come into play—need to be worked out in detail.

Contingencies are thought through, and provision is made for a change of plan should this be required. In the case of totally unexpected events some sort of stabilization plan needs to be prepared.

CHAPTER 41

Orange Gumboots

People Crises and Exercises

When the emergency or crisis involves people, then an understanding of psychology may be required. This may mean understanding the behavior of an individual, certain groups, or certain situations. Understanding perceptions, values, and emotions is important. It is difficult to empathize with people with different personal styles, but this must be attempted. The strategies and psychology of negotiation may be needed. Time and the use of time are important.

In the end most people crises are solved through shifts in perception—either of the reality of the situation or of the future. Changes in perception precede changes in behavior and changes in emotion. Changes in perception are much more powerful than logic arguments. It is necessary to develop perceptions and present the possibility of alternative perceptions. Once an alternate perception is presented, it may not be accepted, but it can't be unthought. Because perceptions are fragile and can easily be destroyed by a false move, it is important for a single person to be in charge.

Where people are involved, then trust, credibility, and personality play a big part. It may be necessary to change the people involved in order to begin a dialogue. Egos, pride, and turf battles are counterproductive when orange mode action is needed.

Exercises

Describe the dangers in each of the following situations, and explain how these dangers might be contained.

❶ A bank robber takes two staff members as hostages and asks for a getaway car.

❷ A tanker carrying gasoline collides with a car in the center of the city, and gasoline begins to leak out of the tanker.

❸ A certain confectionery is found to have been contaminated with a poisonous substance.

❹ A plane is unable to lower one of its landing wheels. There are 200 passengers on board, and the plane is running out of fuel.

❺ An incorrect translation in a recipe published by a national newspaper asks for the use of a poisonous laurel leaf instead of the harmless bay leaf.

❻ A man with a history of mental illness has doused himself with gasoline and is threatening to set himself on fire unless his estranged wife returns to him.

❼ A peaceful demonstration gets out of control and is taken over by violent protesters, who proceed to overturn cars and smash up shop windows.

❽ A toddler who cannot swim is seen to be walking toward a swimming pool. No one is near the child.

CHAPTER 42

Orange Gumboots

Orange Gumboot Action Style

Emergency or crisis action. Accepting the need for orange gumboot action mode. Assessing the situation, the dangers, and the possible developments. Clear sense of priorities, which means removing, containing, or reducing the danger. Everything is directed toward this purpose. Clearly understanding who is in control and the lines of communication. Designing a detailed strategy for action. Planning the steps and also the fall-back positions. Assessing the risks of any action and also the risks of inaction. Using expert help where possible. Assessing the likelihood of success. Putting the strategy into action. Everyone knowing what has to be done and who is going to do it. Periodically reassessing the situation. Modifying or even changing strategy as required.

A main characteristic of the style is focus—on the danger and on ways of reducing that danger.

CHAPTER 43

Orange Gumboots

Summary

Orange is a vivid color suggesting warning and alarm. Gumboots are worn by fire fighters and emergency teams; they are not normal everyday wear. So the orange gumboot action mode is concerned with emergencies, crises, and dangers. Its focus and priorities are clear—reducing the danger. The situation and the dangers involved need to be assessed carefully. A strategy and action steps for carrying through that strategy need to be designed. It is within this tight framework of defined action steps that action takes place. The risks of action and inaction are constantly reassessed within a framework of coordinated action rather than the ad hoc initiative of the brown brogue mode. There may be a range of situations—from those that obviously require orange gumboot mode to those that have some orange elements. Focus, urgency, and sense of priorities characterize orange gumboot action mode. ♙♙

PART VII
Pink Slippers

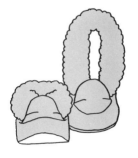

"TREAD CAREFULLY. THIS IS PINK SLIPPER stuff. Imagine you were dealing with your own family."

"She has been with us a long time. She is very loyal. But we do need someone else in that position. Put on your pink slippers, and deal with the situation."

"If we are not careful, a lot of people are going to get very upset. We had better all put on our pink slippers and tread very carefully. If we act clumsily, the whole project is dead."

"Look, muscle does not solve every problem. We know you can manage the muscle bit. Can you also do the other side—the pink slipper bit?"

Pink is a warm color. Pink is a conventionally feminine color: blue for a boy and pink for a girl. Some health-care institutions have pink-colored rooms for patients who are violent or disturbed; pink soothes and calms them.

So the pink action mode has to do with human feelings, compassion, sympathy, and tender loving care. People caring for people is the essence of a family. People caring for people defines a successful community. People caring for people is the basis of civilization.

The human caring values advocated in all religions are in pink slipper mode.

Pink shoes or pink boots are a little absurd and difficult to visualize. Slippers suggest comfort, and humanity fits directly with the pink action mode. It's difficult to visualize being aggressive in pink slippers.

So from the color and from the nature of slippers we form an image of what the pink slipper action mode is all about.

10:30 A.M. U.K. TIME, 2:30 A.M. LOS ANGELES TIME: PAUSE TO SLEEP. AWAKE AGAIN AT 1:00 P.M. U.K. TIME, 5:00 A.M. LOS ANGELES TIME: EVERYONE ELSE STILL ASLEEP. LIGHT INADEQUATE FOR TYPING.

Pink slipper mode applies to all actions involving human feelings and human caring. The police often are involved in situations where they are seen as the guardians of law and order, but they also are heavily involved in a caring role—caring for victims of crime, handling domestic disputes, and dealing with the mentally disturbed.

Medicine and nursing are essentially pink slipper professions, although technology increasingly has shifted the health-care professions' emphasis from caring to scientific understanding. You may understand a great deal about an illness but not care much for the patient. Mother Teresa is a prime example of human caring and the pink slipper mode in action.

Some situations are pure pink slipper mode, but as with the orange mode, many situations have some pink slipper aspects. It is the action mode that most often mixes in with the other action modes—one pink slipper and one orange gumboot.

Wherever people are involved, there is a pink slipper element, but this doesn't need to be specified in every case. Only where a special caring element needs emphasizing does the pink slipper mode need to be spelled out. Many pragmatic situations require one brown brogue and one pink slipper.

CHAPTER 44

Pink Slippers

What Is Caring?

Is caring a matter of sympathy, compassion, and understanding—or the actions that go with these feelings? Some people may be very good at experiencing the feelings but not very good at doing the actions. You may weep with sorrow at someone's distress, but that's not the same as comforting the person. Feeling has value, but not as much as feelings put into action as active caring. Pink slipper mode is not just about being sensitive and feeling the right feelings: it is about action. Of course, it would be difficult to have caring actions without some basis in caring feelings, but feelings are not enough. Indeed, there are some instances where feelings can become almost a self-indulgence for the person with the feelings and not much use to anyone else.

What matters most is not the actual feeling of empathy or sympathy but the intention to care and the actions that arise from this intention. If you see a tragic photograph of a starving child, you may feel sad, but if you contribute to Oxfam, that is an action.

Is it necessary to have a strong understanding of psychology or human nature in order to show caring? Certainly not. Children and simple people show just as much caring as graduates in psychology—probably more. A child who feels sorry for an injured animal cares deeply but may have little psychological sophistication. Caring is a human emotion and not an intellectual exercise.

CHAPTER 45

Pink Slippers

Caring and Action

The use of the pink slipper action mode usually takes one of two forms:

- *Pink slipper mode that adds an element of human caring and human compassion to other actions*: The pink slipper action mode may remind people of the human aspects of a situation. A person who is rather brusque may be reminded of the importance of the pink slipper action mode. In this sense the pink slipper mode modifies other actions.

- *Pink slipper mode as the prime activity*: Comforting victims of an accident may be pure pink slipper behavior. So may be dealing with an unhappy work force or an irate customer. Intervention in domestic disputes is very largely pink slipper in nature.

The caring element may modify actions that must take place, or the caring may be the very purpose of the action. Caring actions are designed to show caring and offer help. The practical nature of the actions will vary with situations, but it includes such fundamentals as the willingness to listen.

CHAPTER 46

Pink Slippers

Training for Caring

People matter. Over the last few years business has learned that people matter. Motivating employees has become a key element in business success. Human resource departments used to have low status but now rank equal to research, production, and similar departments. Businesses promote all sorts of slogans about "putting people first." Scandinavian Airlines (SAS) started the fashion with its reminder to staff that customers paid the wages in the end. Tom Peters in his book *In Search of Excellence* emphasized people, and even though many of the excellent companies in that book subsequently went bankrupt, the focus on human resources makes sense. It has spread to all parts of business and is even beginning to affect government services. Today a variety of formal programs emphasize customer care and also people care within an organization. It is realized that people work better when they are motivated and interested in what they are doing.

Changes in attitude occur in people who view videotapes that illustrate poor customer service. When this sort of behavior is highlighted and caricatured, people tend to avoid it. No one wants to be seen as insensitive.

Caring means what it says. Small gestures can be important. They show that someone matters and that someone cares. Calling people by their name. Remembering who they are and what their interests might be.

Offering help in small ways. Being willing to listen. Inquiring about someone's family. These are all ways of showing people that they are important to you. If you care about someone, then that person is important. Sometimes these sorts of things can become overdone and can appear artificial, but as in so many other cases, abuse of a method does not invalidate that method.

As with all other action modes the simple process of labeling a situation *pink slipper mode* creates a particular framework for action. Action needs are now perceived in a special way. Perception is important: in an orange mode situation you are alerted to the dangers; in a pink mode situation you are alerted to the human aspects. People are very good at playing the game that is required of them at the moment. But the rules of the game have to be clearly spelled out. That is what the six action shoe labeling does. It doesn't mean play-acting, artificiality, or insincerity. It is a reminder of the nature of the situation and the action required. It is a tangible description of the idiom or feel of a situation. It is not simply being told what action shoes to use but telling yourself as a type of shorthand. In fact, the artificiality of the labeling method is an advantage because it sticks clearly in mind: it is more powerful to say, "Use the pink action mode" than to say, "Be compassionate and caring."

CHAPTER 47

Pink Slippers

Levels of Caring

There are several possible levels of caring:

- *Intention:* The desire to care

- *Feeling:* Empathy, sympathy

- *Gesture:* Visible actions that show caring

- *Action:* Actual help and care

It is difficult to generate feelings—the second level of caring—if they don't arise spontaneously. But as many religions have found, it is not always necessary to experience the emotions. Actions can spring directly from intentions. The intention to care may generate pink slipper caring actions even if a strong caring feeling is not present. This is an important realization because you cannot order people to feel caring, but you can ask them to carry out caring actions. If this were not so, then the success of the pink slipper action mode would depend entirely on how people feel at the moment. It would be impossible to do more than exhort people to be more caring.

In fact, even if the pink slipper action mode is carried through almost as a mechanical routine, it still has value.

CHAPTER 48

Pink Slippers

*Interaction with Other
Action Modes*

It is possible to feel sorry for a young person who has gotten into bad company and has been led into crime. How much should this feeling interfere with what has to be done about the crime? The answer is that it should not interfere directly. It is possible to feel sympathy for a person and yet carry through the requirements of the law. If, however, a sole bread-winner is arrested, then it is possible to help the family with welfare or support arrangements. In other words the pink slipper action supports other actions but usually does not run counter to those actions.

At times pink slipper sentiments may clash with the formal impersonality of navy shoe routines. On such occasions it is necessary to explain the need for the routines.

Sometimes, especially in brown action mode, pink slipper considerations may override other considerations because they become a central part of the situation. The pragmatism and flexibility of the brown brogue action mode would usually be sensitive to pink slipper factors.

In general things that need to get done do get done, but humanely rather than inhumanely. That is the pink slipper influence, and it fits with what I indicated earlier about pink slipper mode being a modifier of ongoing actions or a prime action source in itself. Sometimes the main purpose of the action is human caring, and then actions are chosen specifically for that purpose. The priority is human caring just as the priority in orange mode action is reducing the danger.

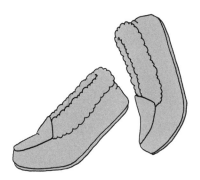

CHAPTER 49

Pink Slippers

Using the Pink Slipper Action Mode

"Someone is going to have to go to tell her that now her second son has been killed in a drug raid. You may feel that these men deserve what they get, but that doesn't apply to the mother. This is real pink slipper stuff. Do your best."

"He has nowhere to go. They threw him out when they discovered he had AIDS. See what you can do with your pink slippers on."

"What about the guys who lose out in this deal? Should we feel something for them? What about some pink slipper action? Is that feasible?"

"People are misinformed, but they are genuinely worried about toxic emissions from this chemical plant. They don't just need better information. They need some pink slipper understanding."

"Sometimes all the pink slipper activity required of you is that you listen. Listening is very much a part of caring."

"These schizophrenics with nowhere to go need medical attention—and also pink slipper attention. So do their families."

"We're going to have to reduce the work force. It's not going to be easy. It's both orange mode and pink slipper. There is no other way out."

"As a leader he is a disaster. He knows what should be done, but he totally lacks pink slipper skill."

"I think these are cries for attention—a way of asking for some pink slipper caring."

CHAPTER 50

Pink Slippers

Monsters

Some people behave inhumanely. The Nazi concentration camps illustrate this possibility. Even brutal guards, however, seemed to show tenderness to their families or their pets. In their perceptions some people draw a line around the real people for whom they should care; outside that line are the enemy—subhumans, animals, and creatures who deserve no consideration. This is a particularly brutal form of the us versus them mentality. The Japanese behaved brutally in their prison camps because honorable people did not surrender and therefore, by definition, prisoners were not honorable and did not need to be treated with respect. Most religions seek to stress our common humanity.

Pink slipper action removes these lines and barriers in order to realize that everyone deserves human care. This is not easy, especially if you come to expect equal consideration in return.

The current business idiom is an attempt to change a perception from "That is a member of the public who must accept what you care to provide" to "That is the customer who really pays your wages."

CHAPTER 51

Pink Slippers

Summary

Pink is a gentle and feminine color. Pink suggests humanity and tenderness. Slippers suggest comfort and domesticity. So the pink slipper action mode has to do with human feelings—with caring and compassion. Feelings go with caring, but actions show caring. Even when the feelings are not there, the actions should be carried through. There are times when the pink action mode is the main purpose of action, as in providing help and care. At other times the pink action mode modifies whatever else is being done so that what is done is done in a humane and caring manner. The pink action mode is always a reminder that people matter. The pink slipper action mode applies to everyone.

PART VIII
Purple Riding Boots

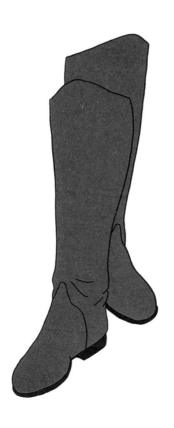

"**A**N OFFICER IS AN OFFICER BECAUSE OF THE officer role. Playing out the purpose of that role is purple boot action mode."

"I'm here in my official capacity—not as your neighbor. I'm wearing my purple riding boots, as it were."

"He never learned how to act as teacher and as friend. He always confused the roles and could never keep order in the classroom."

"Sometimes the mildest of people can act with authority and leadership when they are given an official role. Sometimes they even become tyrants."

"You have an official position. Act out that position. That is what the purple boot action mode is all about."

Purple is a grand color. Purple was the imperial color of Rome. Purple dye was extremely expensive because only a few drops of dye could be obtained from thousands of a particular Mediterranean seashell. Only certain people were permitted to wear clothes dyed with this purple. Purple is also the color of royalty.

Purple is not an everyday color like brown or pink. It has always been the color of pomp and position. So the purple action mode indicates an authority role. People who hold authority positions may act differently in those roles than they do as individuals. Riding boots are not normal wear. People wear them for riding horses or perhaps motorcycles. Once only a few privileged people owned horses. The word *cavalier* comes directly from the word for *horse*, as do the words *chivalry* and *cavalry*. The horseman was a superior fighting person, and in society the superior people who owned horses literally looked down on people on foot.

This type of footwear corresponds with the image set by the purple color: the purple riding boot action mode is all about official positions. An official position is not necessarily a superior one, but when an official acts within the boundaries of that role, then he or she has more authority than someone without an official role. It's no longer the person who acts but the official role. There might even be a conscious separation between the person and the role: "Speaking as a person I admire what you did. Speaking as the principal of this school I am going to have to punish you for violating our discipline code."

The role of a judge is to administer justice. A good judge carries out that role properly, even though in his or her private life the judge may not always act fairly or reasonably.

CHAPTER 52

Purple Riding Boots
People and their Roles

You listen to your doctor because he or she is in an official position and is expected to have expert knowledge and experience. If you ask for a second opinion, you will ask for it from another doctor.

The church used to play a central role in the lives of most people. The vicar or priest was often asked for advice. Before the days of television the village schoolmaster was often the source of all knowledge because books were scarce.

You consult your lawyer because you need an expert opinion about whether you have a strong case for suing your neighbor. You do not rely on your own opinion.

In all the above cases the official role is played by someone with expert training: the doctor has studied medicine, and the lawyer has studied law. Other official roles, however, have no grounding in expert training. A person may be in an official role because there seems to be a need for that role and for having someone play that role. The most suitable person who is eligible or who applies is selected. You may object to the need for that role and to the suitability of a particular person to hold the role, but the role is there and a person is filling it. You may feel that there are too many police officers and that certain people are unfit to be police officers; nevertheless, policing seems to be a necessary function of society.

Society is an organization of people for their mutual benefit. Organizations require that decisions be made and actions be carried out. These needs justify establishing official roles. The will of society, as expressed by elected members of a legislature, is implemented by people performing official roles. Police officers, fire fighters, judges, school principals, and ambassadors carry out the functions of their official roles. Even in communes that actively resist bureaucratic hierarchies people usually perform temporary official roles: someone is in charge of cooking, someone disposes of the garbage, and so on.

CHAPTER 53

Purple Riding Boots

Living Up to the Role

Some argue that no person should hide behind an official role to escape personal responsibility for an action. Activities may be carried out by a person performing a role rather than by that person as an individual.

Some argue that people in official roles should behave as they do in private. So a teacher should be a friend and counselor rather than a teacher and disciplinarian. A tax inspector should be a financial consultant. A police officer should be a neighborhood watchdog. This is a sensible plea for more humanity and more pink slipper action in performing these roles. But taken to extremes it becomes impractical. The official role gives authority and power to some people and not to others: being cautioned or arrested by a police officer is not the same as being cautioned or arrested by an ordinary person.

Actors and actresses are sometimes shy in ordinary life. They enjoy being on stage and losing their personality in the identity of the character they are playing. They pick up one role and put it down at the end of a performance.

Quite ordinary people become judges and quickly learn to act with the wisdom and dignity of a judge. Similarly, ordinary people take on official roles and act with arrogance and tyranny. As I have observed before in this book, the abuse of something does not destroy its value. The petty tyrannies of some officials do not destroy the value of official roles.

The role is bigger than the person because it has been identified by society as necessary. In the purple action mode people can perform actions that might be impossible for them to perform without their role. The role magnifies innate abilities because it clearly defines how a particular ability is to be used.

Navy action mode has a clear guide to behavior: carry out the routine. Grey action mode has a clear objective: collect information and use it. Orange action mode has clear priorities: reduce the danger. Pink action mode has clear objectives: care for people. Similarly, purple action mode also has clear guidelines: act according to the duties of your role. As an actor or actress performs on a stage, the person in purple action mode acts a part.

There is no need to be embarrassed or apologetic about playing roles. Nor is there any value in always being in the purple action mode; that would be both unnecessary and tedious to everyone. But when required, a person should be able to switch into the purple action mode and act with the power and authority of that mode.

CHAPTER 54

Purple Riding Boots
Role and Responsibility

With the power of a role also goes the responsibility of that role. In Japan the head of the airline was expected to resign when one of his jumbo jets crashed into a mountain killing almost everyone on board. He accepted responsibility even though he was not directly involved in the crash in any way. A faulty repair had been made on the plane.

A key and disturbing question about the purple action mode must be addressed. At the Nuremburg trial of Nazi war criminals after World War II many of the accused claimed that they simply were carrying out orders—doing only what their purple action mode demanded. They had received orders and as soldiers carried out those orders. They claimed that just as a soldier could not be tried for murder for killing on a battlefield, so they could not be held responsible for actions that caused other types of deaths. This defense did not apply to all defendants because some instances of personal brutality went beyond the carrying out of orders.

The general principle is that if orders are illegal or criminal then they should not be carried out. If a country enacts laws that sanction behavior others regard as criminal, and if the behavior infringes on human rights or is contrary to a generally accepted concept of natural law (meaning that in most countries it would be illegal), then purple action is no defense. Nevertheless, certain countries have laws that other countries might regard as violating human rights (for example, the death penalty).

No role takes a person above the law—not even the role of President of the United States, as Watergate showed. Nor does any role relieve a person from being a human being first and an official second. The role is an enhancement of the person as a human being and as a member of society, and therefore those performing roles are bound by all the rules, laws, and considerations that apply to private individuals.

If an official role requires you to act according to the laws of society and you still disapprove of the actions your role requires you to take, then you should resign from the role. You also should campaign to change the role's responsibilities.

CHAPTER 55

Purple Riding Boots

Interaction with Other Action Modes

To what extent is the purple action mode similar to the navy action mode? Both are concerned with formal procedures, yet they are fundamentally different. In the navy action mode a routine is performed step by step: a clerk may ask a person to fill out a routine form but has no authority to require that person to fill out the form. In the purple action mode the person performs the role without referring to formal steps. It is almost brown action mode but shaped by the character of the role: the nature of the role guides behavior. In the purple action mode a person can use initiative just as in the brown brogue mode. The navy action mode and the purple action mode overlap when an official carries out a formal routine ceremony.

On occasion there also may be a close synergy between the purple action mode and the orange action mode because the leadership and authority conferred by the role may be useful in emergency situations. When there is no time to establish personal leadership, the official role provides automatic leadership.

The purple and the brown action modes some-times harmonize and sometimes clash. As mentioned above, pragmatic brown action mode may be needed even when in purple action mode. At other times the low-key brown brogue approach may be subverted by an insistence on purple action rights.

The pink action mode may help soften the harshness of the purple action mode. No role is designed to make people inhuman, but the pink mode may remind role players of their humanity. In a clash between the demands of the pink mode and the purple mode, however, the purple normally takes precedence. A judge needs to administer justice even while feeling compassion for the sentenced person.

The grey sneaker mode is sometimes enhanced by the purple boot mode and sometimes inhibited. Sometimes obtaining certain types of information is easier when asking from an official position, but sometimes it may be inhibited by an official role.

CHAPTER 56

Purple Riding Boots
Use of the Purple Boot Mode

"Right now I am acting in my official role—purple boot mode. My sympathy for you doesn't influence my decision in this matter."

"You can't always behave as if you were everyone's best friend. You may end up being resented when you have to carry out your duties. Sometimes you have to make it clear when you are acting in your official capacity. That's what the purple action mode is for—to make this clear to yourself and to others."

"As your lawyer, wearing my purple riding boots, I can tell you that you have a good case against the company. As your friend I must tell you that a lawsuit will take a lot of time and money and will distract you from other things."

"I am asking you to go there wearing your purple riding boots. Go there in your official capacity. It doesn't matter whether people resent this or not. We need an official presence there."

"You wear a uniform to show that you have an official role. There is a certain behavior that goes with the uniform. This is the purple action mode. It has some advantages over being in plain clothes."

"You don't normally go around killing people, but as a soldier in uniform your purple action mode is to defend yourself and your country and to kill if necessary."

"Switching from the purple action mode to the pink mode I am going to give you some personal advice: there's no future in this business. It is better to leave now and find a new job while you're still young."

"Putting on my purple riding boots as head of this family these are the decisions that I'm inclined to make. I'll listen to your views, but I still make the decisions in the end."

"I'm the boss, and I'm firing you."

"In the past I've suggested what you should do. Nothing has happened. Now I'm putting on my purple riding boots, and I'm telling you what to do."

"He has a diplomatic position, and whether we like it our not, we have to treat him in the purple action mode."

CHAPTER 57

Purple Riding Boots

*Carrying Out Purple Boot
Behavior and Exercises*

There are two main requirements for carrying out
purple boot behavior:

- The behavior must be clearly signaled.

- The behavior must be consistent.

If a person is wearing a uniform, then this instantly signals purple action mode. In any case that is
what should be assumed. If the person wearing the
uniform indicates that the purple action mode is being
set aside for the moment, then any return to that mode
must be clearly signaled.

Many people with official roles (school principals,
supervisors, and so on) do not wear uniforms. They
work with people who know their official positions,
but it is important that they clearly signal all purple
boot action. This is even more important when the
person often switches from a formal to an informal
role. Other people need to know unmistakably which
action mode is being acted on at the moment. In time
the phrase *purple action mode* may be sufficient indica-
tion. For the moment the retreat into the official role
may need to be indicated in another way:

> "Personally I see your point of view, but as shop
> steward I have to tell you that the suggestion
> would be totally unacceptable to the union."

Consistency and signaling are complementary. You cannot switch in and out of the purple mode as suits you. How would you feel if your lawyer joked about your professional dealings at a dinner party? It is permissible to make an occasional contrast between what you feel as a person or a friend and what you feel in your official role—but this is done to emphasize that you are in purple action mode:

> "I know your situation very well, but there is no way I can put you ahead of the other people on the list."

Exercises

For each of the following situations indicate how the purple boot action mode could be useful.

❶ Bacterial contamination of a type of meat product is reported in the press. Some people have become ill as a result of eating these products.

❷ A holiday charter flight is delayed for several hours at an airport, and the passengers are becoming very angry.

❸ In a hospital several staff members have had their wallets and purses stolen.

❹ Persistent bullying occurs on a school playground.

❺ A rumor is circulating that a business is in trouble and that several workers will have to be laid off.

❻ A family is shunned in the neighborhood because the son has acquired AIDS from a transfusion of infected blood.

❼ A bitter family dispute has erupted about who should care for an elderly parent.

❽ The incidents of rough behavior and hooliganism are increasing at sports events.

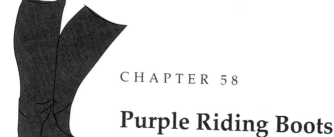

CHAPTER 58

Purple Riding Boots

*Purple Riding Boot
Action Style*

The style is authoritarian but civilized. The role player makes it clear when the official role is being performed. It is necessary to signal this role playing and to remain consistently within the role. The duties, obligations, and expectations of the role provide guidelines for behavior. Behavior is firm, neutral, and fair. Those performing the role don't need their actions to be liked all the time, but tyranny and bullying are unacceptable.

Most important, the person acting in this mode must make clear that he or she is acting out a role and then must behave according to that role. To pretend to assume the role and then to act in a way that is inconsistent with that role leads to confusion and devalues the role function.

CHAPTER 59

Purple Riding Boots

Summary

Purple is an imperial color and suggests authority. Riding boots are used for special occasions. The purple riding boot action mode indicates that a person is acting in the capacity of an official role. An individual is not acting: the role is acting. Indeed, the person consciously acts out the role. Behavior is guided by the behavior expected of that role. It is important to signal this role behavior and to act consistently with the role. Within these limits there is room for initiative.

PART IX
Combinations of Shoes

ONE OF THE ADVANTAGES OF USING THE
shoe metaphor is that we normally wear a pair
of shoes. Although in real life it would be
unconventional to wear one pink slipper and
one orange gumboot, we can combine action
modes when an action seems to call for a response that has both pink and orange elements.

There is no formal framework for combining the
different modes of action. In discussing each of the
shoes I have provided suggestions and examples of
combinations, and I offer more in this section.

1. *Balanced combination:* The situation demands an
   equal measure of two different action modes.

   "This is very much a pink slipper and brown
   brogue situation."

   "I want you to go in there with one purple boot
   and one orange gumboot."

   "We want to make only official inquiries, so one
   grey sneaker and one navy shoe."

   "Make your inquiries, but do it gently—grey
   sneaker with pink slipper."

2. *An uncertain situation:* The balance of action may
   tip one way or the other. Two colors are needed to
   cover the possibilities.

   "At this point I just don't know. Things could go
   either way. Be prepared for brown brogue or
   pink slipper action: carry them both."

145

"When you get there, you may find that it is more purple boot than orange gumboot. It depends on what happens. Be prepared for either."

"Essentially this is a grey sneaker assignment, but it could suddenly become brown brogue if you discover something important."

3. *A modifying situation:* One action mode dominates but another action mode acts as a *modifier*.

"Straight purple action mode, but keep that pink slipper somewhere in the back of your mind."

"Brown brogue. Do what you think necessary. But keep the grey sneaker in mind too. There may be useful information to be picked up."

"Go through the navy shoe routine but with a strong flavor of purple boot in the background."

Here are some potential combinations of action shoe modes. They are simply suggestions: each pair could have several overlapping definitions.

Navy and Grey: Routine and formal inquiries.

Navy and Brown: Routine behavior with the possibility of being flexible and using initiative if necessary.

Navy and Orange: Routine procedure in an emergency.

Navy and Pink: Routine procedures carried out in a gentle manner.

Navy and Purple: Routine procedures with the weight of an official role behind them.

Grey and Navy: Investigations using formal procedures such as checklists.

Grey and Brown: Investigations using initiatives and ad hoc action to obtain more information.

Grey and Orange: Investigations in dangerous and sensitive situations, such as infiltration and undercover assignments.

Grey and Pink: Investigations using a sensitive and considerate manner to obtain information.

Grey and Purple: Investigations using an official position to collect information.

Brown and Navy: Practical action that uses flexibility and occasionally routine procedures, even personal routines.

Brown and Grey: Practical action that is sensitive to information in order to determine the next action step.

Brown and Orange: Practical action in a dangerous or potentially dangerous environment.

Brown and Pink: Practical action in a sensitive human situation where feelings and emotions are involved.

Brown and Purple: Practical action dealing with different officials and therefore requiring the use of an official position.

Orange and Navy: Using standard procedures in an emergency.

Orange and Grey: Collecting expert opinion and as much information as possible regarding an emergency.

Orange and Brown: Practical moment-to-moment action in a rapidly changing emergency situation before planning becomes possible.

Orange and Pink: Dealing with human suffering in an emergency.

Orange and Purple: Dealing with officialdom in an emergency; deciding who is in charge.

Pink and Navy: Using routines for dealing with delicate situations involving feelings and emotions; can be personal routines.

Pink and Grey: Listening and noting in order to offer help and comfort.

Pink and Brown: Practical action and initiatives in helping people.

Pink and Purple: Using official channels and positions in order to help people.

Purple and Navy: Formal behavior as part of an official position.

Purple and Grey: Using official statistics and information channels.

Purple and Brown: Practical action and individual initiatives within the framework of an official position.

Purple and Orange: Giving orders and organizing in emergencies; leadership in a crisis.

Purple and Pink: Modifying impersonal official behavior with human sensitivity.

It is also possible to have flavors of more than two colors in a situation, but doing so begins to dilute the effectiveness of the method.

In practice situations are rarely pure examples of one or another action mode. There is no need to specify all possible combinations. It is usually enough to indicate the dominant action mode, even when the situation is not pure. 👣

PART X
Action, Not Description

It is IMPORTANT TO REALIZE THAT THE SIX action shoe framework is not intended as a description or classification of action. The purpose of the framework is to set the *style of the action* in advance so that a person can behave within a certain style framework. You keep in mind the required action style and try to fit your actions to that style. The purpose is not to describe actions after they have happened or to analyze behavior.

This is an important point because the limited framework of the six action shoes is inadequate to describe complex actions but is suitable as a style framework. If it contained any more shoes, the framework would be too complex to be usable. It is pointless to offer guidelines for action if they are not practical.

Establishing a practical framework for action (as in the six hats and the six shoes) does not derive from the traditional academic exercise of analyzing for description's sake. I want to help you *do* something— not analyze what has been done. The purpose of the six action shoes is not to categorize people or behavior, as in "This is this type of behavior" and "This is another type of behavior." They are not analytical descriptions of behavior but style suggestions for behavior: they are concerned with what is about to be done and not with what has been done.

Some people operate better in one or another action mode. Some people feel more comfortable operating in one or another action mode—as in the pink mode rather than the purple mode. But the action modes should not be used to categorize people. Each person must be capable of operating in each of the different modes, just as with the six thinking hat framework each person must be capable of using each of the six hats. If this principle is not firmly adhered to, then people sink back into a category ("I'm a brown brogue person") and never attempt to develop other action skills.

The strong and natural tendency to use the six action modes for purposes of description and categorization must be resisted because it destroys the value of the system as a style framework for action. 👣

PART XI
Simple and Practical

SOME PEOPLE WANT LIFE TO BE COMPLICATED. **They believe that uncomplicated approaches can't be serious or worth much. When I talk to educators, I sometimes become aware of an interesting Catch-22 situation that goes something like this:**

"Please make your talk so complicated that we shall be impressed—but unable to use it."

In other words, if it's not complicated, it can't be serious enough to use. But if it's complicated, then it's too complicated to use.

Some people are suspicious of simple things. They view something like the six hat method or the six shoe method as simplistic and childish because it is easy to understand. Yet experience has shown that the six hat method is extremely powerful, which is why it is now being used widely by many of the world's largest corporations. Simple things are usable.

I make no apologies for the simplicity of the six shoe method. If you try it, you will find that it is practical and that it works well.

It is not easy to suggest that a person behave in a particular way. People may be offended if you tell them to behave in a more caring way. The six shoe framework is neutral and offends no one. The framework can be seen as a game or ritual. People find it easier to follow the rules of a game than to change their personalities. The colors and physical nature of the shoes make them easy to visualize and remember.

PART XII
Language and Terminology

I HAVEN'T BEEN RIGOROUSLY CONSISTENT IN
using terminology for the six pairs of action
shoes in this short book, and I have a reason for
not doing so. The six action shoes can be referred to in a number of different ways, and I
have used these various terms in my descriptions of the shoes in each section.

When you introduce the concept of the action
shoes, it is important to emphasize both the color and
the physical nature of the shoes. This imagery should
be reinforced from time to time. You can't imagine just
brown, but you can imagine a brown brogue. You can't
imagine pink, but you can imagine pink slipper. Each
style of shoe further reinforces an action style. The
metaphor loses its power if you start off talking about
pink action or orange action. From a perception point
of view, it is important to emphasize both color and
style.

Once the idiom has become firmly established,
however, it can be cumbersome to refer to the full title
of the action mode: *purple riding boot action mode* is
quite a mouthful. A number of shorter ways can be
used to express the same thing. These are inter-
changeable:

"Put on your purple riding boots."

"This is purple action mode."

"Use purple boot behavior."

"Let's have some purple action now."

All these expressions can be used for each shoe.
Use a variety, and change them around. The weakest is
simply to use the color, as in *purple action*. Referring to

an approach as *purple action mode* gives it more formality and clarity.

With some of the action shoes one type of expression may seem more appropriate than another. With the orange gumboots it seems appropriate to talk about an *orange action mode* because it implies danger (like a red alert).

The expression *brown brogues* may sound natural to some people, but others may need to be shown what a brogue type of shoe looks like. After the explanation the expression can be used directly: "This requires brown brogue action."

The term *pink* cannot be left hanging in midair and does not naturally correspond to any particular situation. Visualizing slippers adds considerably to the meaning of this action mode. The idea of slipping into pink slippers also suggests a gentle and sensitive approach. We can then talk about a *pink slipper situation, pink slipper action,* or *pink slipper action mode.*

The combination of grey with sneakers is not incongruous, but in some countries *sneaker* may need to be defined as *tennis shoe, gym shoe,* or *running shoe.* Referring to *grey situations* is misleading. Even the expression *grey action mode* might be misleading. It is best to keep the combination of *grey sneakers,* as in *grey sneaker situation, grey sneaker action,* or *grey sneaker action mode.*

The term *navy shoe* or *navy action mode* may not evoke any particular situation, so we talk about *navy shoe routine* or *navy shoe formality* to reinforce meaning.

Purple riding boots can be shortened to *purple boots,* although the riding boot metaphor should be described at least once because there are so many other types of boots that do not make the same point. So we might say, "This is a purple boot situation" or "This is purple action mode." The color purple is quite strong by itself and can give a direct sense of the official meaning underlying this action mode.

In time shorthand expressions will be used. From time to time, however, it is important to refer to the full name of the action mode in order to maintain the vividness of the imagery. This imagery is important for the ritual associated with mentally putting on the shoes. The more deliberate and artificial this ritual, the more powerful the technique. The imagery also underscores the distinct identity of each action style and avoids having them blend into one general style and losing all value.

Remember always that the styles of *action* are being characterized and not the situations themselves. Referring to a *pink slipper situation* means that a situation requires using the pink slipper action mode.

The framework itself can be referred to in a number of different ways:

"Six pairs of action shoes"

"Six shoe action framework"

"Six action modes"

Using the term *shoes* is an important part of the imagery, so don't be timid about using it because you feel it doesn't sound serious or scientific. The awkwardness soon passes, and the usefulness of the term remains. It is less effective to talk only about action modes or colors of action modes. ••

4:47 P.M. U.K. TIME, 8:47 A.M. LOS ANGELES TIME, 4:47 A.M. NEW ZEALAND TIME: END OF TASK. BOOK IS COMPLETED. TWO HOURS AND TWENTY-NINE MINUTES TO ARRIVAL IN AUCKLAND.

7:16 A.M. NEW ZEALAND TIME, 7:16 P.M. U.K. TIME: LAND IN AUCKLAND.

PART XIII
Action Mode
Summary

CHAPTER 60

Action Mode Summary

Navy Formal Shoes

Color navy blue. Formal shoes. Navy suggests routines, drills, and formality.

Navy action mode is for routine behavior. Select the appropriate routine, switch into the routine, and carry through the routine as perfectly as you can.

Routines are crystallizations of the best way of doing something. They remove the need to think something through each time. They reduce the risk of error.

Go through the routine systematically step by step. Use flexibility if you absolutely have to, and return to the routine as soon as you can.

Routines can be improved and may need changing, but that is a separate action. Don't seek to improve a routine while you're using it.

Although they may appear restrictive in some ways, routines are also liberating because they free you to think about other matters.

Once you have switched into the navy shoe action mode, then apply the routine as perfectly as possible.

CHAPTER 61

Action Mode Summary
Grey Sneakers

Color grey. Sneaker type of shoe. Grey suggests grey matter of the brain. Grey also suggests fog and mist. Sneakers are quiet and casual.

Grey sneaker action mode is for collecting information and thinking about it. That is its prime objective. The style is low key and unobtrusive. The information is used to clear up the fog and mist suggested by the color grey.

Sometimes information can be collected in a systematic way by creating a procedure and then following it. Sometimes established routines can be followed.

At other times it may be necessary to have a hunch, a theory, or an hypothesis to start collecting information.

Collecting information may lead to a theory or hypothesis that then leads to further information collection.

The purpose of information collection is to be as comprehensive and neutral as possible: it is not to support your initial hypothesis.

It is a good habit to keep at least two hypotheses in mind to avoid being led astray by one hypothesis.

The final stage of information collection is to check out the most reasonable hypothesis. Avoid clinging to a single hypothesis too early.

CHAPTER 62

Action Mode Summary

Brown Brogues

Color is brown. Brogue type of shoe. Brown is the color of earth, and the action style is down to earth. The brogue is a hard-wearing shoe suitable for most occasions.

The emphasis is on pragmatism and practicality. It is a matter of doing what can be done.

Moment-to-moment adjustment and flexibility in response to the situation are called for.

Have a clear sense of objectives and priorities.

Behavior is guided by objectives, priorities, and basic values and principles.

Behavior is determined by personal initiatives at the moment rather than by formal routines or master plans.

Be sensitive and respond to the situation, but keep in control and don't just follow.

Effectiveness and simplicity are important. The purpose of any action is to be effective.

Choose from and combine existing action patterns. Do the obvious unless surprise has some particular value.

CHAPTER 63

Action Mode Summary

Orange Gumboots

Color orange. Gumboot style of footwear. Orange is the color of danger, fire, and explosions. Gumboots are worn by fire fighters and emergency crews.

Orange gumboot action mode has to do with emergencies, crises, and dangerous situations.

When situations are unstable, unpredictable, and likely to get worse, urgent action is required (if only to get medical attention).

Action usually is needed, but in special cases involving people waiting may have a strategic value.

The clear objective is to reduce the danger. This may require attending to the source of the danger or removing people from the danger area.

Determine who is in charge, and establish communication between the different parties involved.

A strategic plan needs to present carefully worked out steps.

Everyone must know what is to be done and who is doing what.

Backup, follow-through, and fallback considerations are required.

Flexibility is necessary if the plan does not work according to expectations.

Obtain as much information and expert advice as possible.

Assessment and reassessment of the situation are vital.

Emotions are usually heavily involved.

Courage is needed both in making decisions and in taking action.

It always is easy, in hindsight, to say how things could have been better.

Action Mode Summary

Pink Slippers

Color pink. Slippers as a style of footwear. Pink is a gentle, feminine color. Slippers represent comfort and domesticity.

Pink slipper action mode is concerned with human caring—with sympathy, compassion, and help.

Feeling is not enough. The feeling must be put into action.

If the feeling is not there, the intention to act in a caring way still results in caring actions.

The prime consideration is that people matter as people.

Caring applies to all people. Some people are not worth more caring than others.

Listening is an important part of caring.

Sometimes caring is the prime purpose of the action. At other times the pink slipper action mode may be used to modify, in a caring direction, other types of action that are taking place.

Understanding the perceptions and values of others is a key part of caring. Understanding precedes appropriate actions.

CHAPTER 65

Action Mode Summary

Purple Riding Boots

Color purple. Riding boots. Purple is the traditional color of authority, as in ancient Rome. Riding boots suggest a special function.

Purple riding boot action mode has to do with authority and playing out an official role.

The person using the purple riding boot action mode is not acting as a normal person but through an official role that he or she is performing.

Actions must be consistent with the duties, obligations, and expectations of that role. Within this framework initiatives are possible.

Signal to those around you when you switch into the purple action mode and are going to be acting through your official role.

Once you have indicated that you are acting in an official capacity, be consistent and don't keep switching back and forth between official and unofficial roles.

Purple action mode can be modified by pink slipper considerations, but duties must be performed.

There is no obligation to perform duties that are illegal or immoral. ♥

For information on becoming a certified licensed trainer based on Dr. de Bono's *Six Thinking Hats* and *Six Action Shoes* concept please write:

Diane Smith
International Center for Creative Thinking
805 West Boston Post Road
Mamaroneck, NY 10543